Liturgy, Justice and the Reign of God

Integrating Vision and Practice

Frank Henderson
Stephen Larson
Kathleen Quinn

PAULIST PRESS
New York/Mahwah, N.J.

Book design by Celine M. Allen.

Library of Congress Cataloging-in-Publication Data

Henderson, Frank (J. Frank)
    Liturgy, justice, and the reign of God: integrating vision and practice/ Frank Henderson, Stephen Larson, Kathleen Quinn.
      p.   cm.
    Bibliography: p.
    ISBN 0-8091-3050-5: $9.95 (est.)
    1. Catholic Church—Liturgy. 2. Christianity and justice. 3. Kingdom of God. 4. Sociology, Christian (Catholic) I. Larson, Stephen, 1949–
   . II. Quinn, Kathleen, 1951–   . III. Title.
BX1970.H345   1989
264′.02—dc19

                       88-31690
                       CIP

Published by Paulist Press
997 Macarthur Boulevard
Mahwah, New Jersey 07430

Printed and bound in the
United States of America

Contents

Acknowledgements

More than twenty colleagues in the fields of social justice, liturgy and religious education, from four Churches, critiqued the first draft of this book. The book was also "field tested" by three groups of people who studied liturgy and justice with Stephen Larson one winter. In addition, it was discussed at length by the Study Group on Liturgy and Justice of the North American Academy of Liturgy. We are extremely grateful to all these people—too many to name individually, unfortunately—for their time and invaluable comments, even though it resulted in the writing of a new chapter and a major reworking of the format of the book as a whole.

This process of consultation was both humbling and empowering. The three of us were privileged to put into form the painful questions and experiences of many. We hope that we have also faithfully recorded their reasons for hope.

We dedicate this book to our spouses:
Ruth, Rebecca, and John,
and to our children:
Katherine and Sarah Larson, and
David and Brendan Kolkman-Quinn

1. Introduction

The celebration of the risen Christ by the assembly of believers is one of the most effective political actions [people] can perform in this world—if it is true that this celebration, by contesting any power system which oppresses [humankind], proclaims, stirs up and inaugurates a new order in the created world.

Joseph Gelineau[1]

We address this book on social justice and liturgy first to our sisters and brothers who are deeply committed to social justice, and who work hard on social justice issues, both part-time and full-time.

Many of you find it very difficult to believe or accept Joseph Gelineau's statement about the justice-relevance of the regular Sunday liturgy of the church. Some of you are angry at the church because it does not seem to support your interest and commitment, your work for social justice. Sunday worship is, for you, part of this negative experience. Many of you are angry because church life—within worship and elsewhere—seldom seems to embody social justice values. Others of you have given up on the worship of the church and rarely participate in the Sunday liturgy.

We share your anger and your disappointment. And we challenge you to move beyond anger and disappointment to share the vision of justice linked with worship.

We address this handbook also to our brothers and sisters who are deeply committed to liturgy, and work hard on worship matters, both part-time and full-time.

Many of you also find it difficult to affirm Gelineau's statement. Some of you have had negative experiences of "peace liturgies" or other thematic worship imposed on Sundays that has produced more guilt than praise. Some of you have been alienated by social ministry emphases that seem

I visited one of these banned people, Winnie Mandela. Her husband, Nelson Mandela, is serving a life sentence on Robben Island, our maximum security prison. I wanted to take her Holy Communion. The police told me I couldn't enter the house. So we celebrated Holy Communion in my car in the street in Christian South Africa. On a second occasion, I went to see her on a weekend. Her restriction order is more strict at weekends. She can't leave her yard. So we celebrated Holy Communion again in the street. This time Winnie was on one side of the fence and I on the other. This in Christian South Africa in 1978.

Desmond Tutu[2]

1

"What are these for?" asks an out-of-town visitor as she stands in the gathering area of St. Joseph's Church here. "These" refer to two big baskets at the back of the church. As people come for Sunday eucharist, many come bearing a loaf of bread, or some filling for sandwiches. Whatever is brought, is taken up at the offertory procession in the basket as a sign to all of sharing our daily bread with those who might not have daily bread.

It's 5 p.m. Outside the rectory door a group is gathering waiting to come inside for their evening meal. These evenings there are more than 40 people who come for supper. The front office in the rectory has been converted into what looks like a small diner—complete with booths and benches. (The food collected, offered and blessed during the liturgy is now ready to be shared.)

St. Joseph's Parish, Ottawa, Ontario[3]

distant or removed from a biblical foundation. Some of you have perceived a gap between the church's life of prayer and its mission and ministry. Some of you have invested so much energy into improving and renewing Sunday worship that the connections to daily life and ministry have become diminished. Still others of you have failed to appreciate fully the connections between liturgy and daily life, or have seen worship only in terms of personal piety.

We share your hope that worship will center, uphold and animate our lives of faith. And we challenge you to share the vision of liturgy lived out within a mission and ministry of social justice.

We address this book especially to our sisters and brothers who are excited about the theory and vision expressed by Gelineau, but who have seldom actually experienced this in your own regular worship life, or who are not sure how to put it into practice in your own congregation. Whether lay person or ordained minister, you often find yourself isolated and alone in your concern that a relationship between liturgy and social justice be expressed clearly and faithfully Sunday by Sunday.

We would like to assist and encourage you at this very practical level.

We address this manual finally to our brothers and sisters who are reasonably content with the liturgical life of your parish and are satisfied with its social justice ministry. Some of you do not understand the dynamic relationship that exists between liturgy and social justice. Others of you do not understand what the concern is all about or do not care about it.

We would like to open your eyes.

We do share the vision expressed in Joseph Gelineau's statement. Furthermore, we believe that the relationship between social justice and liturgy is not artificial, contrived, secondary or imposed, but rather is completely intrinsic to the very nature of both of these facets of the Christian life. Finally, we believe that the theory, vision and highest expectation that the church holds regarding its worship expresses this relationship naturally. Thus we believe that there is no need to make radical alterations in the liturgical vision of the church, though indeed some refinements are required. Instead, there is a great need to clearly understand this liturgical vision and to live it creatively and faithfully in our Sunday by Sunday practice.

Our Aims

Our aims in this handbook are threefold:

(1) To provide a practical study guide to help people discover the connections between liturgy and social justice;

Church Architecture Offers Message to Neighborhood

There are three churches in my neighborhood.

I don't attend any of them, which means I see them only from the outside. But if I decided to go to one, their outsides might help me decide which one, because they present very different faces to the neighborhood.

One is a large, white pillbox. It rises at least two storeys and in winter, when the sun is low, it casts its shadow into yards halfway down the block.

One can see the people entering and leaving the building, but no one can tell what they do inside. There are a few windows around the entryway, but the upper half of the building and a long wall along the back alley have no windows.

Another of the churches has no more windows, but a lower architectural profile. In front is sometimes one of those portable lighted signs, with paste-up letters, telling people what's going on: a film series, a children's program, a women's Bible study.

The third is my favorite. It's the smallest, a congregation of a mainline denomination which is not particularly noted for its emphasis on neighborhood outreach or special programs to offer. But one thing this church building has is windows. They are large clear windows, along the walls of the sanctuary, and anyone looking at the church from the outside can view right into the worship area.

I imagine that this congregation plans some day to put stained glass windows where the clear glass is now. I hope they don't. There are too few churches around, in spite of all the hype these days about evangelism and outreach, which reach out to the community with the very building in which they worship.

These churches' architectures deliver very different messages to those outside the sanctuary.

One, the big white pillbox, suggests that its celebrations are not public celebrations. No one can see what happens behind the walls. To be part of them, one must enter the building, become part of the "group."

The second church welcomes the neighborhood through its sign, although the building itself offers no special welcome.

The third building says: "We have no secrets. When we worship, pray, sing, you can see what is going on. If you join us, you already know what we do."

There is a new church going up in my neighborhood. The foundation is in and the framing is going up. I wonder what kind of statement this church will make, even before the congregation moves in.

Paul De Groot[4]

---

(2) To provide a practical aid to improve liturgical practice so that the intrinsic connections which exist between liturgy and social justice will be better expressed within the liturgical celebration; and

(3) To provide an aid for communication among liturgists, social justice people and religious educators, especially with a concern toward bridging the gap between theory and practice in the parish regarding liturgy and social justice.

This manual is intended to be accessible to an ecumenical audience whose basic pattern of worship is word and sacrament, with baptism at Sunday worship on occasion. It would readily lend itself to adaptation to those communities whose practice reflects diversity such as word only, occasional eucharist and baptism infrequently.

It is, however, something of a primer. It attempts to provide an introduction for worshiping communities to relate liturgy and social justice. As a result, it is relatively brief, seeks practical application and does not attempt to say everything on the subject of liturgy and social justice. An extensive list of resources is included to encourage and direct those individuals or communities who desire further study and analysis. In addition, a brief bibliography is included for those whose reading time is limited.

The Lamp

Mark 4:21–25

This gospel we heard at a Mass on Mancarroncito, the last and most remote island of the Solentiname Archipelago. The Mass was at the home of Dona Yoya, under an arbor. We came to Mancarroncito because it is far removed from the rest of the archipelago, and those who live there, very poor and with very few boats, can seldom get to our little church.

FELIX said: "I think the gospel is a very high doctrine that God has offered to humanity to give us all light. That's why it's like a raised lamp." Someone from Mancarroncito: "Jesus never went around hiding. That's the light on high. And we have to be like that, too. Not hide with the truth but bring it out into the light."

JULIO MAIRENA: "People who have hidden justice are the ones who hide the light. Christ came for the poor. But often the priests, because they're getting the money of the rich, have hidden this message for the poor. And that's the light under the bushel, under the grain basket. There are others who, through fear of the powerful, apply the gospel only to their private lives, and that's the light under the bed, it seems to me. The one who raises the light high is the one who protests against injustice."

FELIPE: "Not only the priests. We also hide the light. We also have the duty to preach the truth, and many times we don't speak it out of fear. And we have to speak the truth, even though they threaten us, or attack us, or kill us, as has always happened with the prophets."

REBECCA said: "The lamp is Christ. Because he said: 'I am the light.' Anyone who reads it and then hides the book in a drawer is hiding the light. Anyone who reads it and then tells about it to someone else is bringing out the light so it can be communicated to another neighbor . . ."

FELIPE: "We make that light shine with friendship, making one island friendly with another. Putting an end to separation and the isolation that there is on our islands . . . We communicate Christ when we communicate friendship. The light, then, is love."

The Gospel in Solentiname[5]

Format and Content

Through most of this book, the text is accompanied by resource material. The text is divided into eight sections:

1. Introduction
2. Liturgy's Call to Social Justice
3. Principles of Liturgy and Social Justice
4. The Gathering of God's People
5. The Liturgy of the Word
6. The Liturgy of Baptism
7. The Liturgy of the Eucharist
8. The Sending Forth of God's People

Thus after three initial chapters, we simply follow the outline of a full Sunday liturgy. As we consider each part of a Sunday worship service, we begin with a general discussion of the relationship of that part of the liturgy to social justice. We then go on to consider what is actually done in each part of the liturgy, and its significance for our subject. In this more practical section, we deal both with the verbal and the non-verbal dimensions of Sunday worship.

One focus of this handbook concerns the liturgy's verbal language. The verbal dimensions of the liturgy are abundant. They include poetic biblical texts spoken or sung; dialogue between presider and assembly; prayers voiced by the people; songs which bear at times lament, at other occasions joy and praise; words which voice our confession and from which we receive forgiveness. Chiefly, the verbal dimension of liturgy's communication revolves around story telling, as God's story of redemption and salvation is proclaimed from biblical text, prayer, or with a preacher's insight. Inclusive language with reference to people is a significant motif of social justice. Similarly, a broad range of images of God is essential to articulate the full biblical scope of God's self-revelation. We are aware that the language of quoted texts is not consistently inclusive. Many of these passages were written when consciousness of this issue was different than it is today. In some cases emendation was precluded by copyright considerations.

Non-verbal dimensions of the liturgy are another focus for our consideration, for they also communicate the relationship between worship and social justice. Some examples of these non-verbal dimensions would include: architecture; the environment of worship; signs and symbols amidst the assembly; the full participation of people in sharing the ministry of worship; the presence within the assembly of children, the aged and infirm; music and silence.

Questions are interspersed throughout each section to help you reflect on your own feelings, experiences, and understandings. The questions should also serve to assist you to consider specific actions that might be appropriate in response to what you have read and upon which you have meditated.

The resource materials are related to the text, especially liturgical texts from official worship books now in use in several churches, and quotations from various contemporary writers on liturgy and social justice. Brief citations are provided for the resource materials. More complete bibliographical information may be obtained following the last chapter.

How To Use This Handbook

We hope that this book will be used, first of all, for study and reflection by individuals and groups. As an individual you could simply read through it. You will want to take care to think about the questions you encounter in light of your own experience with liturgy and social justice.

Groups within a congregation could also make use of this book. If it is a small, intimate group, the gathering could share in leading the discussion. If it is a larger group, you will want to designate someone to facilitate the process of working through the study guide. The questions for reflection throughout could be considered by individuals or in small groups before reporting back to the larger group.

Whether used by individuals or groups, it is essential that worship form and inform your reflection. As you use this manual, continue to let worship be a central part of your life. Your

"Credo" for a "Bread" Service

I believe that bread comes from grain
that grows in the wind
and the rain
with the farmers' help
far from the eyes of city folk.

I believe that bread comes from love
the love of (God)
the love of the farmer
the love of the baker's hands
the love of those who bring it to me.

I believe that bread can be and should be
broken
and shared
and given to all persons
until all have enough
and then some.

I believe that Jesus loved bread
and took it
and broke it
and blessed it
and fed his disciples
and asked them to feed us
forever.

I believe enough in bread
to want it from Jesus
to want it to nurture me
to want his life through it
to want to give life through it.

I believe that his body as bread feeds me
and as part of his body
I want to be bread for others.

I believe the Spirit will help me
as will Jesus' people. Amen.

Bread for the World[6]

worship life will itself help to focus, critique and illustrate your consideration of this book.

Study and reflection can include the general principles regarding social justice and liturgy that we express, and also how the book relates to your own personal experience of Sunday worship. Here we hope that the questions posed throughout the text prove useful, provocative and challenging.

We hope that such study and reflection will be useful before, during and after each Sunday liturgy. Before, as an aid in worship planning; during, as an aid to ministers and congregations as they worship; afterward, as a guide for evaluation leading to better worship the following Sunday.

Chapters 4 through 8 consider the five components of the fullest form of Sunday worship: gathering, word, baptism, eucharist and sending forth. We realize that baptisms will in practice be celebrated only on occasional Sundays, and that in some denominations or churches the eucharist also is not celebrated every Sunday. Nevertheless, we present all five elements for the sake of completeness, and because all should be present every Sunday at least as memory and expectation.

In writing these chapters, it is not our intention simply to convey intellectual knowledge in an abstract fashion. Instead we hope to engage you, the reader, at a personal, lived level and to challenge you to action. Our aim is thus to be practical and applied, leading you and your worshiping community to change your practice both of worship and of social justice ministry.

Thus, at regular intervals throughout these chapters we ask you to stop: reflect on and digest the material, allow yourself to be both challenged and affirmed. This process is very

---

If You Have Time to Read Only a Few. . . .

A. Books

Brown, Robert McAfee. *Unexpected News: Reading the Bible With Third World Eyes.* Philadelphia: The Westminister Press, 1984.

Hellwig, Monika K. *The Eucharist and the Hunger of the World.* New York: Paulist Press, 1976.

Hessel, Dieter T. (ed.). *Social Themes of the Christian Year.* Philadelphia: The Geneva Press, 1983.

Hovda, Robert. *Dry Bones: Living Worship Guides to Good Liturgy.* Washington, D.C.: The Liturgical Conference, 1973.

Searle, Mark (ed.). *Liturgy and Social Justice.* Collegeville: The Liturgical Press, 1980.

Willimon, William H. *The Service of God: How Worship and Ethics Are Related.* Nashville: Abingdon Press, 1983.

B. Articles

Egan, John. "Liturgy and Justice: An Unfinished Agenda." *Origins,* Vol. 13, No. 15, September 22, 1983, pp. 245–253.

Hovda, Robert. "The Mass and Its Social Consequences." *Liturgy* 80, June/July, 1982.

Kiesling, Christopher. "Liturgy and Social Justice." *Worship,* Vol. 51, No. 4, July, 1977, pp. 351–361.

Lathrop, Gordon. "The Eucharist as a 'Hungry Feast' and the Appropriateness of Our Want." *Living Worship,* Vol. 13, No. 9, September, 1977.

Searle, Mark. "The Pedagogical Function of the Liturgy." *Worship,* Vol. 55, No. 4, July 1981, pp. 332–359.

Seasoltz, R. Kevin. "Justice and the Eucharist." *Worship,* Vol. 58, No. 6, November 1984, pp. 507–525.

Wren, Brian. "Justice and Liberation in the Eucharist." *The Christian Century,* October 1, 1986, pp. 839–842.

Factory

Our congregation is concerned about the use of resources. We believe church buildings are not sacred sanctuaries, but rather places for God's people to meet and to use in response to community and world needs. These concerns have implications for the kind, use, and size of buildings which become our meetinghouses.

In early years, our congregation met in a variety of places—a lounge on a college campus, the stage of an auditorium, a doctor's waiting room, a dance studio which stood vacant on Sunday, and a winterized pavilion in the local park.

Eventually we wanted a building of our own to expand congregational life and community ministries. What kind of building should it be? We didn't want to invest heavily in real estate and wanted a building that would be multipurpose.

After months of searching, we bought a one-story, 13.5 × 33 meter (44 × 110 foot) factory building. The initial cost was $34,000, though some renovations will need to be made.

One section of the building is to be used as an apartment, where a household will be living to supply the presence of members in the building and community and to facilitate ministries we hope to develop. The entire building is available during the week for congregational and community needs. Two good possibilities are daycare for kindergarten children and emergency housing. The larger open area of the factory will serve nicely as a meeting place for worship and celebration.

It's an adventure in faith to recycle a factory for kingdom use!

Assembly Mennonite Church[7]

---

important, whether you read this just by yourself or together with others. We urge you not to skip over these parts of the book, but to carefully consider them.

Each of these five chapters follow the same general pattern, which consist of four sections. The first section is quite brief. It simply describes how each part of the Sunday liturgy typically is conducted. We then ask you to describe what *you* actually do on Sunday morning in your own congregation. This allows us to take into account the variation in practice that quite legitimately can occur from place to place, Sunday to Sunday, and from denomination to denomination. It is also helpful for you to reflect upon and to name your own actual practice and experience. But all of this should not take too much of your time.

The second section presents our understanding of the relationship between each part of the Sunday liturgy and social justice. We present this as the *vision* that comes from the wisdom and best experience of the Christian tradition from the time of Christ (and even before) to the present time. Because this is a *vision,* we say things such as: "Our gathering is characterized by joy and hope." "The word proclaims the reign of God," "The eucharist is a meal for hungry people," rather than "The liturgy *should be* this or that." If you are uncomfortable with the gap between the "is" of our vision and your own actual experience, that is good! In fact, you should be uncomfortable with our vision, for we are as well. It both challenges and informs our practice.

We then ask you to reflect on the relationship between liturgy and social justice that you actually experience in the worship of your community, as well as upon your own understanding of what this relationship should be.

What Language Shall I Borrow?

We need worship resources that confront and comfort us with the Christ who was a poor Galilean and walks beside us even in apparently hopeless situations.

A first step in selecting worship resources is to look at the current body of hymns with fresh eyes. When we look at familiar hymns we may discover those that are most appropriate to have a continued honored place in our worship. Next we must discern those hymns whose enculturated patterns may be less appropriate for today. Finally, we can look to resources beyond our own culture to find new hymns that speak to us in our current needs.

The step of weeding out inappropriate hymns is more painful. Each of us holds dear some hymns which are less suited for corporate worship today. Certainly, any one particular hymn may be quite appropriate for our own private devotions or in a small group of close friends. However, when the worshipping community is more diverse the problems of hymn choices are multiplied.

The third step in this process of hymn choice is a positive and crucial step. Fewer hymns are available unless we add new hymns. However, by removing less appropriate hymns we make room for new appropriate hymns in worship. Many new resources are becoming available to us. If we refuse to give up any of our past, we have no room to grow.

We hinder the coming of God's kingdom when we too readily accept the comfortable resources of our own culture. We often prefer the path of least resistance where those who worship within our sphere of leadership feel comfortable. We must sometimes choose a prophetic stance that helps us grow in faith and worship praxis.
Mary Pope[8]

The third and fourth sections then consider the actual liturgical celebration in some detail. The non-verbal and verbal dimensions of each part of the liturgy are dealt with separately. We have tried to name the components of a typical Sunday liturgy, realizing at the same time that variation occurs in practice. We also point out how the general vision enunciated in the second section of each chapter might be lived out concretely in your congregation.

Questions within and following these final sections have in part to do with your understanding of the relationship between liturgy and social justice as this is expressed concretely in the course of Sunday worship. In addition, we ask you to evaluate your own experiences of worship, and to name aspects that are good and those that need improvement.

We suggest that you spend several sessions working through this handbook; perhaps you or your group could take one chapter at a time. Such a procedure would also allow for Sunday worship to intersperse your group's discussion. The Sunday liturgy would then become a worthy resource for you to reflect upon, critique and evaluate as you study the dynamic relationships between liturgy and social justice.

Practical Implementation

We are very much concerned that the use of this study guide lead to concrete action in your own local congregation. In no place is the practice of social justice, liturgy or their relationship perfect. Therefore, in every place these can be improved. We want you to take your learnings and your reflections home. Use them to make changes in the social justice and liturgical life of your church community. Because there is no other good opportunity to do so, we would like to expand on this point here and make several reflections and suggestions on how this practical application might be carried out.

Whether as individual small or larger group, the following types of process might be followed, with appropriate modifications depending on the type of group, its concerns, interests and responsibilities, and the time available.

Analysis

Analyze the Sunday liturgies of your own congregation, with the help of the content of this manual and the questions included in it.

From the point of view of the relationship of liturgy and social justice:

● What is good about your Sunday worship?

● What is acceptable but could be improved?

- What aspects of these liturgies "sin by omission"? That is, what fails to speak to the relationship of worship and social justice, but does not actually contradict the principles involved?

- What aspects "sin by commission"? That is, what either constitutes poor social justice practices themselves, or directly contradicts the relationships between worship and social justice described in this study guide?

Action

Based on the analysis you have carried out, decide various courses of action. Affirm and support good practices and the people who are responsible for them. Make a list of what most needs to be improved, in order of priority. Make a list of what can most readily be changed, in order of priority. Decide, in each case, what needs to be done to effect each change. This may lie in the area of general education of the congregation, worship committee, and/or ministers; the process of planning the liturgies; ministry and other aspects of the services themselves; encouragement and affirmation within the community.

Additional considerations may include: How can you assist in making changes by personally volunteering your help? What depends, in whole or in part, on other people? Who are they? How shall they be recruited and motivated? How can you effectively express your concern to them? How can you influence them to make changes? What pressures—people, structures or budget—are working against these changes either implicitly or explicitly? How can these pressures be diminished?

In light of these questions, develop a plan of action and set goals for six months, one year, two years and five years. If certain changes will cost money, develop a realistic budget and consider where this money will originate.

Evaluation

As you do make changes in the liturgical life and social justice ministry of your congregation, find out how people feel about these changes. If possible, respond helpfully to any negative reactions.

You might ask the following types of questions: What did you like about the changes? What helped you to worship better? Did anything make you feel uncomfortable or hinder your worship experience? What and why? Are the changes making connections for you between worship and social justice? Are you feeling that your worship life is present and active in your social justice ministry?

Remember to invite and truly hear the responses of all segments of your congregation, including children, young adults, people who are alone and those who are elderly.

In considering the implementation of ideas and sugges-

I do not feel that I am alone in this sense of alienation in our society about certain forms of liturgical practice. Maybe I am more critical than others. . . . One such occasion was a midnight mass. That Christmas the beautiful "U-shaped" church had white (artificial) Christmas trees located all around the dark brick walls. There probably were 30 poinsettias around the altar. The robed choir was on chairs and sometimes stood between the altar and the people. They had a carol concert before mass, and several "selections" during the Eucharist including solos and duets. The singing was excellent. I am sure that everyone left the service on a high. I found myself leaving on a low. It was a turn-off for me. I never was a great Christmas person. Perhaps it's the melancholy which Christmas carols cause me. Perhaps it's because I am a childless person. I felt myself being angry in what I felt was a high celebration of middle class values and culture.[9]

Another example (of alienating liturgies) is more of an ideological nature. (There was a major ecumenical event to mark a national social justice program.) It was held in the largest gothic church (in the city). A few hundred people turned out, not bad if it had been held in a smaller church. The church had regimental colours hanging from the ceilings. All the robed church leaders were gathered in the sanctuary, backed by a robed choir, which sang polyphonic music. The beautiful Spanish songs were sung by a small group of Canadians (!) There were a handful of Central Americans in the congregation. The excellent address on the Church and Central America was given from the high pulpit. This rich old man turned away sad, because the whole atmosphere militated against the message![10]

In a Salvadoran village, a group of women and men take turns hoeing beans on their cooperative farm. The co-op is a new venture. Its aim is to help local people improve their livelihood and to reduce their dependence on a few exploitative produce merchants. As they hoe, they sing and laugh, while young children dart among the rows of beans. . . . Several days later, the tortured bodies of two co-op members are found beside a road leading out of town.

The Ploughshares Monitor[11]

tions presented in this manual, and in bringing about changes in your congregation's worship, remember that there are people involved. Some of the members of the congregation will not understand what you are trying to do or why, or will be opposed to it. Others simply will not like it. Yet they are still your sisters and brothers in Christ.

Remember that you are dealing with worship, a central act of the church and for many the principal activity of their church lives. You will think you are improving it; others might feel you are tinkering with it in arbitrary and irreverent ways. You will think that change is good; others might think that it is not even permissible or possible to change the church's worship.

Consider that social justice issues usually are difficult and painful to encounter. They concern matters about which some people would just as soon not think, into which they would rather not put their energy. They may concern topics that involve emotions and raise strong feelings, which some would wish to avoid. Social justice values may threaten the lifestyles and ways of thinking of some of those present. Social justice considerations almost certainly will divide people. Yet again, the community is made up of brothers and sisters in Christ. How will you raise these issues in a caring and pastoral manner that invites growth and change?

Be aware that to attempt to better express the intrinsic connection between worship and social justice is much more than just to fix up what is done and said during one hour on

Liberals Being Frozen Out of Church

A recent poll by Maclean's magazine found that among those dissatisfied with their church, most thought it was too conservative.

According to the poll, 65 percent were pleased with their church's position on social and political issues, 24 percent thought it was too conservative, and eight percent thought it was too liberal.

That eight percent sure makes a lot of noise.

We're often led to believe churches are failing because they've mixed their religious and social agendas, becoming too concerned with things of this world. They are losing the "old time religion" which, in the mythical golden past, attracted wagonloads of families, dressed in frocks and their best suspenders, every Sunday.

I suspect we hear more complaints from conservatives because they stay in the church, convinced it has values they will find nowhere else. Liberals don't complain; they leave, convinced that what little they are getting out of church can be found elsewhere. (Both are wrong, but that's another story.)

The notion, popular even in churches, that religion deals with the "spiritual" person and everything else belongs to the secular realm, has not helped. Those concerned about social issues, about contemporary society and trends, are not merely pulled into secular activism because they hope to find answers and opportunities to participate; they are pushed by their own churches, which agree that such activities are somehow peripheral to the spiritual life, and tell them: "If you want to end poverty, be a social worker."

Another reason liberals leave the church may be its sheer lack of imagination. For some, Sunday services are a place of rest and refuge, one of the few things in their life which has not changed in 10 years. Others, particularly those not part of the network of personal relations in a congregation, find unimaginative church services stultifying. It's not surprising they look for something better to do on a Sunday morning. And find it.

Paul De Groot[12]

The Multiplication of the Loaves

Luke 9:10–17

OLIVIA: "Jesus was pleased to have those humble people with him listening to his word and that's why he hadn't wanted to send them away. Maybe he didn't want them to give too much importance to food, more importance than to his word. And those people who had gone to seek probably weren't thinking of food. Maybe they didn't even feel hungry hearing his word."

JULIO MAIEWNA: "The apostles think there isn't any food, and it seems to me that that's the way we are now. We all say we don't have any food. But it seems to me that the problem isn't that there's no food. It's that a few people have it all. If it was all shared around we'd all be eating what those few who have the food are not eating, and I think we'd all have enough."

PANCHO: "I'm just catching on to what this means here! They didn't have enough—right?—to feed the five thousand people. But then he says to them: it doesn't matter, share it. And there was more than enough! He made them understand that no matter how little they had they had to share it. And they shared it, and with his power he made it stretch out. The lesson is that no matter how little we have we always have to give."

MARCELINO: "Jesus also teaches us that with a little we can do a lot. He doesn't look down on poverty; he uses it to change it into riches. He didn't want to make a miracle without using anything. He didn't say: 'Hell, with those rolls and those herring you can't do anything!' No, he took them and shared them so we could see that with just a little we can do a lot. Here in Solentiname what do we have? A little corn and some fish. . . . But we can make a miracle."[13]

Sunday morning. You are even more concerned with the way people live their Mondays and Tuesdays. For some this can be even more threatening.

Bear in mind that those who misunderstand or object to the changes you wish to make are, basically, people of good will and fellow Christians. Remember that you are not perfect, that you may not be explaining things clearly and convincingly, that you may even make mistakes. To effect change in human lives involves humility and patience on your part.

Reflect upon the fact that you probably were not born with an intense interest in social justice, or a clear vision of the relationship between justice and liturgy. Most likely you grew in these perceptions, you underwent a conversion to your present position as part of your own personal experience and life journey. Other people, with different experiences, learnings, or gifts, have come to other positions and priorities, or are at stages of faith journeys different than your own.

How then might you assist other people to take a further step on their life journey, to undergo a conversion similar to your own in terms of liturgy and social justice? There are no simple, foolproof answers, but a few approaches may be suggested.

Be gentle, but be persistent. Do not attempt too much all at once, but assume your overall plan will take a considerable period of time. Take at least a three to five year perspective; a persistent effort over that period can accomplish a great deal, though perhaps not everything.

Attempt to understand and appreciate the different gifts, experiences and visions of others. Seek to understand what prevents them from sharing your vision. Encourage them to meet their own worthwhile goals, to develop their own gifts. Share your concerns and visions in ways that are as non-threatening as possible, and seek the help of others in achieving them. Include them and try to give them ownership of the changes you are trying to make. Do not appear to dictate to them or force things upon them. Avoid the temptation to impose a "guilt trip" on them, but honor their gifts and nurture their growth.

Remember that more is concerned than intellectual understanding, though education certainly is very important. Carry out your educational efforts in ways that are suitable to adults. Quality liturgical experiences are also very important. Take people to visit other churches where there are worthy practices, so that they may encounter alternative, positive occasions of worship. Help people experience the pain of those wounded by the violation of social justice principles. Assist those in prayer groups and Bible study groups to broaden their agendas to include social justice concerns.

Community is essential; you cannot do it all by yourself. You need to work with others, for the sake of support and continuity as well as because the magnitude of what you wish to accomplish is enormous. It may threaten to overwhelm you if you undertake the task alone.

And finally, keep your sense of humor. Remember that until the reign of God fully comes, our worship will never be perfect. At best it is a kind of dress rehearsal for the feast to come.

2. Liturgy's Call to Social Justice

We are writing about *liturgy*, about *social justice*, and especially about the relationship between these two dimensions of the Christian life.

Yet to some, the relationship between liturgy and social justice is not very close at all—or at least not apparently so. They may say, "What's there to write about?"

To others the question may be, "Why? What's so important about this relationship that it's worth so much paper and ink?"

And still others may say, "We haven't heard much about this liturgy-social justice relationship before. Is this just another new—and passing—fad?"

Or some may say, "My ministry is Christian education. Why should I be interested in learning about the connection between liturgy and social justice? What does this have to do with me?"

And others will say, "I work hard on social justice issues all the time, and liturgy doesn't seem to have much to do with my concerns. Why should I be interested in this subject?"

We would not be surprised at such questions, and we wish to respond to them at least briefly before proceeding to the subject of the book itself.

Stated more broadly, our concern is the relationship between worship and life, especially between that one hour (or so) on Sunday morning and the other 167 hours of your weekday life.

This has been a matter of great concern to thoughtful, religiously committed people throughout Christian—and Jewish—history.

Though in Sunday worship we in a certain way step aside from the ordinary round of daily activities, yet in other ways the two dimensions of religious—and human—life are meant to be intimately connected.

We believe in the God of love, who calls us to reject all idols and who seeks a deep communion with us.

We believe in the God who is not remote but who is immersed in the life of this world sharing its hope and feeling its pain.

We believe in the God who identifies with the poor and the oppressed and those who long for faith and who calls us to stand with them.

We believe in the God whose love is vulnerable, whose heart is aching and whose covenant with all people is unshakeable.

Christian Conference of Asia News[1]

14

Meditation Based on the Beatitudes

People who do not hold tightly to things are
   happy, because all of God's kingdom is
   theirs.
People who are gentle with the earth will
   see it blossom forever.
People who can cry for all the world's
   suffering will live to see happiness.
People who hunger and thirst for what is
   right will finally have their fill.
People who really care will find love
   wherever they go.
People who don't let the world get them
   down will see God.
People who make peace happen are God's
   children.
People who give up their own comfort so
   that others can be helped know what
   heaven is all about.
Lord, let us be like these!

The Empty Place[2]

Middle Class Means Rich

Being personally acquainted with people living on the poverty level provides a tremen-
dous balance against the strong "You owe it
to yourself" and "You deserve it" philoso-
phies so ever present in North America.

Once in Vietnam a missionary family
recently returned from furlough praised the
Lord for his generosity in providing a new
air-conditioner and friends who had outfit-
ted them in better clothing than they would
ever have bought themselves. A Vietnamese
co-worker, listening in, wondered why the
Lord was barely providing enough food for
his table or money to educate his children!

Mary Martin, Allentown, Pa.[3]

If Sunday worship does not connect in some way with our experiences during the preceding week, then something is wrong. And if Sunday worship does not make a difference to our daily lives during the week that follows, something is wrong as well. If such connections are not made—without distorting the quality of stepping aside that worship should also be— then what is the point of going to church on Sunday morning?

Each age has understood and named the relationship between worship and daily living in a slightly different way, using concepts, thought patterns and language appropriate to the time.

Today a very important way of naming this relationship (though not the only one) is to use the terms *liturgy* and *social justice.*

Social justice, then, most broadly has to do with a view of God, of the Christian people and indeed of all humanity, and of the world. More specifically, today we focus not only on ourselves as individuals, but also ourselves as social beings in our contemporary "global village."

To explore this matter in more detail, let us consider who we are who come to worship and what we bring with us; something of what happens during worship; and the transformed life that we are called to live afterward.

In our journeys of faith we bring our whole lives to encounter God in worship; we bring our joys and sorrows, our questions and musings, our crises and hopes.

Joys and sorrows are familiar companions on the journey. It is perhaps easier to reflect upon our joys being brought to worship. It seems natural for us to offer God our praise and thanksgiving amidst joyful occasions: at the birth of a healthy child, surrounded by the wonder and beauty of God's good creation or when love blossoms.

But sorrows are also born into our lives and borne to God in prayer. At times when our spirit is broken and crushed, we also have a natural tendency to turn to God to seek healing, wholeness and comfort: at the death of a child, when a relationship is broken or when we feel abandoned and alone.

Everything of life, our joys and sorrows, is brought to worship.

Questions and musings arise in our experience of life. From our earliest days, it seems, our vocabulary is shaped by question words: Why? What? How? When? Those are the words that are guaranteed to drive the parents of a four year old to the bounds of sanity. But those very questing words reveal a true side of our humanity. We are questing creatures who seek to understand. The book of Genesis images that quest in a story of forbidden fruit. As those first human creatures reached for the tree of knowledge, so we reach out in our questionings and musings to understand ourselves and our world. Our questions deepen and darken as they are shaped by our

One of the great misfortunes of the question-and-answer method of the old catechisms was that people's real experiences were ignored. Not denied—merely discounted. The right answer was what mattered. It did not matter that one had not yet experienced the question. Even more important, the questions coming out of people's lived experience were generally not the questions which the catechism answered.

This is probably a perpetual problem for religion. Many of the truths of religion deal with what we ought to do, the way we ought to be, and the kind of answers we ought to give to life's big questions. But the oughts cannot be understood until there has been some serious reflection on experience. . . .

None of the resurrection stories in the gospels begin with answers. They all begin with the women's wonder and fear, the disciples' confusion and doubt—qualities which the Baltimore Catechism hardly considered virtues. And yet, in the New Testament, these are the raw experiences out of which the disciples' lived experience of the risen Lord began to take shape.

This suggests that there is something very normal and indeed orthodox about the experience of confusion and doubt. . . .

Tad Guzie[4]

---

experiences: Why do we spend billions of dollars on weapons when most people of the world are hungry? Why do women sleep at night on steam grates in large cities of very rich nations? Where was God in an age when Jewish children were handed chocolates by guards as they were led to Treblinka's gas chambers? Our questions echo the questions of Job: "Why do the wicked live, reach old age, and grow mighty in power?" (Job 21:7). Our questions repeat the questions of the Psalms: "Why dost thou stand afar off, O Lord? Why dost thou hide thyself in times of trouble?" (Psalm 10:1). Our questions bring to our remembrance Jesus' last agonized question from the cross: "My God, my God, why hast thou forsaken me?" (Mark 15:34).

Everything of life, our questions and musings, is brought to worship.

In our day, it seems especially that crises and hopes shape our lives. The story of worship and crisis that is recounted in Isaiah 6 provides an example of somewhat similar time. The incident described there took place in a time of profound crisis: in the year that King Uzziah died. The death or unexpected change of a political leader is often a time of crisis and uncertainty. Such a transition can signal a movement toward new and unfamiliar directions. Israel in 742 BCE was no exception, so Isaiah went to the temple during that time of crisis to worship and to pray, to find therein some security, some familiar footing in a time of shifting events.

We gather for worship in a similar time of crisis. The crises of our age are not necessarily due to the death or change of political leaders. Instead, our crises are due to awesome convulsions and changes in human history.

Our crises have to do with war and rumors of war. Twice in this century there have been wars that engulfed the whole world. Regional wars have starkly shaped our geographical vocabulary: Korea, Vietnam, Kampuchea, El Salvador, Iran,

Recycling Is Natural

The order of creation is remarkable.
Nothing disappears completely.
Fire and wood
turn to heat
smoke
carbon.
Leaves become humus for future growth.

The order of people
leaves much to be desired.
We do not honor the earth,
leaves to humus to trees.
We drop our litter,
our aluminum
our glass and plastic
and hope it will disappear.
God watches our folly
and waits for us to realize
his world needs protection
and responsible care.
Recycling is consistent
with God's plan.
Am I part of the order of creation?

Judith Mattison[5]

16

Consumers' Prayer

throwaway bottles
throwaway cans
throwaway friendships
throwaway fans

disposable diapers
disposable plates
disposable people
disposable wastes

instant puddings
instant rice
instant intimacy
instant ice

plastic dishes
plastic laces
plastic flowers
plastic faces

Lord of the living
transcending our lies
infuse us with meaning
recycle our lives

Joyce M. Shutt[6]

In a Cairo slum, a mother cradles a whimpering infant in her arms. The child has diarrhea—the result of impure water—and is severely dehydrated. She will probably die within hours, since the parents have no money for medical care. Three older children, pale and thin, huddle together in the corner of their small shack. Several kilometers away, at the seaport, a new shipment of military transport trucks is being unloaded onto the docks.

The Ploughshares Monitor[7]

Iraq and Afghanistan are names that bring to memory the horrors of war.

Our crises have to do with the technological transformation of war. There once was a time when war affected only the warriors; now warfare threatens the entire creation. The majority of earth's people have been born since 1945. That year designated a critical change in human history. Those born since 1945 have never known a time unthreatened by nuclear bombs. Social psychologists have observed that to live in the shadow of such destructive capabilities profoundly affects people. Indeed, the looming presence of nuclear destruction may be a factor in many societal disorders: family breakups, chemical abuse and dependencies, increased suicide rates, mounting despair or paralyzing indifference.

Our crises derive as well from astonishing technological developments in other spheres of life. Biological engineering, in vitro fertilization, transplants—a baboon's heart beating in a human infant's body—and other medical marvels have challenged our ethical, moral and theological understandings. Chernobyl and the explosion of the Challenger space shuttle have caused us to stop and wonder to what extent we trusted or even idolized our technological capabilities.

Our crises involve the environment. Pollution has eaten away at our planet. Acid rain falls gently upon the lakes of Ontario and Quebec, gradually turning them into lifeless bodies of acidic water. Chemical depositories have leaked disease and death into community water tables. Chemical defoliants used in the Vietnam war have left portions of the Vietnamese landscape barren and hundreds of Vietnamese people barren of life and hope, dying of cancer. In the wake of nuclear testing in the South Pacific, women are now described as giving birth to "jelly fish babies."

Our crises involve unjust distribution of food and other goods. North America is so well fed it is dangerous to our health. Spas and diets interest many North Americans. Our garbage disposals consume more food in a week than many people in the southern hemisphere eat in a month. Malnutrition, famine and starvation are known too well in too many parts of the world. As with war, hunger has shaped our geographical awareness: Ethiopia, Bangladesh, the Sahel, Biafra and Calcutta.

Our crises derive from political and economic ideology. The arms race is a consequence of political and economic differences. Because of the enormous amounts of money diverted away from education, housing, health care and food toward military armaments, the arms race is already killing people before any bombs are detonated. Political differences prod terrorists, inspire torturers and motivate assassins. Economic pressures and ideologies enslave the developing world in debts so massive that interest payments alone cripple entire nations.

Our crises derive from racism. This century is scarred by deliberate and systematic destruction against racial, political and cultural groups. Jews, Armenians, Ukrainians, black South Africans and Namibians, Vietnamese, Kampucheans, native peoples of Guatemala and the Timorese of Indonesia have been among the victims. Humankind's past and continuing inhumanity one to another leaves one speechless and stunned.

The list of crises could go on and on. You may want to spend some time reflecting upon and naming the crises you observe in your own community, within your nation and around the world.

Yet with crisis there are hopes: it seems that we move and dance between crisis and hope. The crisis of war animates our hope for peace. The crisis of hunger compels our hope that all may be fed. The crisis of nuclear arms propels our hope for nuclear disarmament. The crisis of death moves us toward our hope in the resurrection to eternal life. The crisis of injustice flames our passionate hope for God's justice. The crisis of abused children and battered women cries out for the hope that all may be loved, honored and know mercy.

Everything of life, our crises and hopes, is gathered into worship.

King Uzziah is long dead. But the crises symbolized by his death are a constant companion to humankind. In the face of such crises, like Isaiah, we fairly stagger to our contemporary temples to worship and to pray. Like Isaiah, in our time of crises, we go to worship. We can learn from Isaiah's experience.

First, he encountered God: "I saw the Lord . . ." (verse 1). Second, he saw a vision that revealed something of the

My Friend's Four Sons

The four sons of my friend heard me say,
    and repeat:
"This box of chocolates is for the four of
    you . . .
one, two, three, four.
Have you heard?"
When I gave the box to the youngest,
saying once again that it was for all,
the little one opened it,
and, pressing it to his chest, exclaimed:
"It's mine, it's mine!"
I felt as if I had just witnessed a meeting of
    the powerful of the earth.

Helder Camara[8]

Spiritual Closeness to the Land

For thousands of years this culture of yours was free to grow without interference by people from other places. You lived your lives in spiritual closeness to the land, with its animals, birds, fishes, waterholes, rivers, hills and mountains. Through your closeness to the land you touched the sacredness of man's relationship with God, for the land was the proof of a power in life greater than yourselves. You did not spoil the land, use it up, exhaust it and then walk away from it. You realized that your land was related to the source of life.

The silence of the bush taught you a quietness of soul that put you in touch with another world, the world of God's spirit. Your careful attention to the details of kinship spoke of your reverence for birth, life and human generation. You knew that children need to be loved, to be full of joy. They need a time to grow in laughter and to play, secure in the knowledge that they belong to their people.

The old ways can draw new life and strength from the Gospel. The message of Jesus Christ can lift up your lives to new heights, reinforce all your positive values and add many others which only the Gospel in its originality proposes. Take this Gospel into your own language and way of speaking; let its spirit penetrate your communities and determine your behavior toward each other, let it bring new strength to your stories and your ceremonies. Let the Gospel come into your hearts and renew your personal lives. The church invites you to express the living word of Jesus in ways that speak to your aboriginal minds and hearts. All over the world people worship God and read his word in their own language, and color the great signs and symbols of religion with touches of their own traditions. Why should you be different from them in this regard, why should you not be allowed the happiness of being with God and each other in aboriginal fashion?

John Paul II, in Australia[9]

Psalm of Praise

How grateful we are, O God,
    for our great country.
    for the blessings you lavish upon our
      land.
How concerned we are, O God,
    that our very nation may become our
      god
    and that we worship the gifts
    rather than the Giver!

Is it possible, O God,
    that our laws may circumvent your will
    that our freedom may place chains on
      others
    that our wealth may impoverish some
    that our power may come by way of
      another's weakness?
that our enemies may be those
    who are obedient to you?
Dare we pray, O God,
    that you take away those things that
      come between us and you?

Leslie Brandt[10]

**Marginalisation: A Universal
Phenomenon**

Anyone who has stood by the road trying to
hitch a lift in a hurry and watched the mo-
tor cars flash past him, can understand
what is meant by 'marginal'.

A marginal person is someone who is
left by the wayside in the economic, social,
political and cultural life of his country.

They might be immigrants who have
come to look for work, old-age pensioners,
the unemployed.

Marginalisation does not only affect
groups or individuals. There exist today
marginal countries or even continents. This
is what we mean by the 'third world', Africa,
Asia and Latin America.

Helder Camara[11]

nature of God: "Holy, holy, holy is the LORD of hosts" (verse
3). This also revealed something of what God's creation and
God's people are supposed to be. Third, in response to his
vision, Isaiah understood that things are not what they should
be; people are not who they should be. His first words are
of confession: "Woe is me. I am lost; for I am a person of unclean lips and I dwell in the midst of a people of unclean lips"
(verse 5).

Though we often think of "confession" as a very personal,
interior matter, in fact it is much broader as well, the acknowledgment of an ever expanding circle of less-than-perfect
realities. Not only oneself, but also the local church community, and the national and universal dimensions of the people
of God—are not what they should be. Not only oneself, but
also the local civic, social and economic communities, and then
their national and international expressions—are not what
they should be. It is not so much "confession" in the traditional
sense, but acknowledgment of the true state of things and of
people as well. If Isaiah was moved to confession and self-
criticism in these senses, then that should be instructive for
us as well. For in worship we should similarly be moved to
confession and self-criticism for ourselves, our church and our
society.

In response to Isaiah's confession, a seraphim flew to him,
touched a burning coal to his lips, and declared: "Your guilt
is taken away, and your sin forgiven" (Isaiah 6:7). It was then
that Isaiah heard the call from God: "Whom shall I send?"
"Here am I! Send me," responded Isaiah (Isaiah 6:8).

Isaiah stood in faithful continuity with Israel's covenant
with God. His response to God's call was a ministry that, in
turn, called Israel to faithfulness, to remember and to live
God's justice in their lives. Isaiah spoke to Israel's joys and
sorrow, their crises and hopes. He called them to renewed understandings of what it meant to be in covenant with God.
Among those understandings was the call to link their worship
life with life beyond the sanctuary, to join their liturgy to lives
of social justice in the community:

    Is not this the fast that I choose:
    to loose the bonds of wickedness,
    to undo the thongs of the yoke,
    to let the oppressed go free,
    and to break every yoke?
    Is it not to share your bread with the hungry
    and bring the homeless poor into your house;
    when you see the naked, to cover him,
    and not to hide yourself from your own flesh?
    Then shall your light break forth
    like the dawn,
    and your healing shall spring up speedily;

Ambulance Drivers or Tunnel Builders?

A group of devout Christians once lived in a small village at the foot of a mountain. A winding, slippery road with hairpin curves and steep precipices without guard rails wound its way up one side of the mountain and down the other. There were frequent fatal accidents. Deeply saddened by the injured people who were pulled from the wrecked cars, the Christians in the village's three churches decided to act. They pooled their resources and purchased an ambulance. Over the years, they saved many lives although some victims remained crippled for life.

Then one day a visitor came to town. Puzzled, he asked why they did not close the road over the mountain and build a tunnel instead. Startled at first, the ambulance volunteers quickly pointed out that this approach (although technically quite possible) was not realistic or advisable. After all, the narrow mountain road had been there for a long time. Besides, the mayor of the town would bitterly oppose the idea. (He owned a large restaurant and service station halfway up the mountain.)

The visitor was shocked that the mayor's economic interests mattered more to these Christians than the many human casualties. Somewhat hesitantly, he suggested that perhaps the churches ought to speak to the mayor. Perhaps they should even elect a different mayor if he proved stubborn and unconcerned. Now the Christians were shocked. With rising indignation and righteous conviction they informed the young radical that the church dare not become involved in politics. The church is called to preach the gospel and give a cup of cold water. Its mission is not to dabble in worldly things like social and political structures.

Perplexed and bitter, the visitor left. As he wandered out of the village, one question churned round and round in his muddled mind. Is it really more spiritual, he wondered, to operate the ambulances which pick up the bloody victims of destructive social structures than to try to change the structures themselves?

Ronald J. Sider[12]

---

your righteousness shall go before you,
the glory of the LORD shall be
your rear guard.
Then you shall call,
and the LORD will answer,
you shall cry, and the LORD will say,
Here I am (Isaiah 58:6–9).

God, then, in the course of worship, calls us to social justice, and we have to respond. Some are called to what might be called explicit social justice ministries, for example, using their gifts as instruments of God's peace, or in extending God's dominion of justice into all the world. Others, however, hear God's call to employ their gifts in education, to teach people about God's presence in human history. Some see God's call to use their gifts in spiritual formation, to form people who live their baptismal faith with grace and purpose. Others feel God's call to offer their gifts in various ministries of service, music, healing, pastoral care or counseling.

Whatever explicit ministry to which one might be called, *all*—we repeat, *all*—are also called to respond to the call to some kind of social justice ministry. What do we mean? Even if we are religious educators or pastors or parents, we are also called first of all to *see* that things are not the way they are supposed to be, and then to *care* passionately about this. All are called to pray, to contribute financially, to affirm and support those with explicit social justice ministries. All are called to act justly and promote justice wherever we are, in our church

God's School

Give all you have.
Give all you are.
Give yourself always unstintingly.
Joy and peace
to those who love the earth
and they receive
God, three persons who share
and are fulfilled in unity.

Helder Camara[13]

Lord, Try Us

There are those
whose being
is possession.
There are those
whose essence
is giving.

Helder Camara[14]

Weekly Poverty Meals

We lived in Samaru, Nigeria for eleven years. Two years ago when we moved to Kansas we were concerned that our children—then ages ten, eight, and two—be brought up feeling close to the problems faced by people in other countries. As an agricultural economist with a major interest in international agriculture, David was especially eager that we do something together weekly about world hunger. As a result, once a week our family has one supper which excludes meat, fish, milk and dessert. Our meal may be a starch and a vegetable, rice with a little egg, or broth with bread. After about two hours we may have a cup of coffee or tea. We each put forty cents into a globe bank, accumulating this for a nutrition project to alleviate malnourishment among the world's poor.

Linda and David Norman[15]

Trading In the Cadillac

A suburban church in Wichita, Kansas, Eastminster Presbyterian, had launched a $525,000 building program when earthquakes hit Guatemala, destroying thousands of homes and buildings. Many communities were devastated.

At a meeting of the board of elders a layman spoke up. "How can we set out to buy an ecclesiastical Cadillac," he asked, "when our brothers and sisters in Guatemala have just lost their little Volkswagen?"

The elders agreed to modify the building program drastically. They paid the architect and settled for a $180,000 alternative. Then they sent their pastor and two elders to Guatemala to find out just how they could help believers there.

The team reported to the board of elders. They, in turn, with the enthusiastic backing of the whole congregation, borrowed $120,000 from a local bank and used the money to rebuild twenty-six churches and twenty-eight pastors' houses in Guatemala!

Inspired by the example of Eastminster, another congregation modified building plans and sent $60,000 to Guatemala. And a church in India, hearing about the project, raised $1,200 for Guatemala relief!

Waldron Scott[16]

community, in our work, recreation, social life, in our civic and economic communities.

In the liturgy, then, we are called to social justice and empowered by God to mission and ministry. For we, too, like Isaiah, stand in the tradition of God's covenant which graciously draws us into relationship and sends us forth as instruments of God's peace, justice and reconciliation.

But there is a another movement to this symphony. For in the course of our social justice ministries, we return again and again to liturgy to find nourishment, renewed strength and sustenance.

To be involved in social justice issues is to journey into terror and stormy seas. Issues of social justice will take us to places we may not want to go. We will see things that will indelibly remain in our mind's eye. To be involved in social justice is to encounter the broken and crushed dreams of humankind; it is to know women, men and children woefully misused; it is to confront the principalities and powers.

Such a journey should not be undertaken alone. We will need community. We will need others with whom to rage and weep over humanity's plight. We will need companions with whom to bear the burdens of social justice. The word "companion" means etymologically "one who eats the same bread." We will need others to share the same bread, most especially the bread of life.

It is in the liturgical assembly that we will meet such companions to share the journey. Within the community at worship we will encounter the foundations of social justice as God's word is proclaimed, God's forgiveness declared, Christ's body and blood shared.

That community will not yet be the kingdom of God. As Isaiah reminded us, the first word is one of confession, criticism, condemnation of ourselves and the people of whom we are in the midst. The liturgical assembly will not provide a model of perfection or easy answers to social justice woes. But it will hold up a vision of what might be, a vision of that for which we long:

> We need to create situations in which the word of God, both in its verbal form and in its sacramental shape, sinks deeply into our minds and hearts. Then we will begin to see, against the horizon of God's promised kingdom, the flaws in our society, in our church, in our workaday world, and even in our liturgical celebrations. When we criticize our social and ecclesial life from the higher viewpoint of God's word, then we can begin to hear the call to social justice in the liturgy and be empowered by it. . . . The liturgy is the efficacious call to social justice which is available to us.[17]

It was a very good conference
. . . for all the Catholic dioceses of Western Canada.

The conference started exactly the way it had planned,
and it carried on exactly as it should carry on,
until it was discovered that
among the more than two hundred participants,
there was only one Aboriginal person
or maybe two or three,
which was very few for the whole of Western Canada.

The ministers of Social Justice, and the Canadian Bishops
   also,
have said for a long time
that we must see the world with the eyes of the poor and
   the oppressed.

So the next meeting of the dioceses of Western Canada
will be dedicated to listening to the Aboriginal people who
   have been oppressed for over 300 years.
Their history and their stories concern the factory workers,
   the B.C. lumberjacks, the unemployed,
the weary immigrants, the Atlantic fisherfolks, the Prairie
   farmers,
the wondering teenagers, the disabled people, and women
   also.
As we all share our experiences of oppression,
we'll discover that together we can create paths of justice.

. . . And then I awoke, and realized that I was only
   dreaming.
But dreams can come true, can't they?

Rene Fumoleau[18]

Liturgy calls us to social justice. Liturgy serves as a foundation for social justice. Liturgy strives to model God's gracious dominion, to empower our ministries. Such a vision stands behind this book. For we write not so much of what the liturgy *is* but what it might be: a sign to the people of God's gracious reign and a source of social justice in our time:

> Into the liturgy the people bring their entire existence so that it may be gathered up in praise. From the liturgy the people depart with a renewed vision of the value-patterns of God's kingdom, by the more effective practice of which they intend to glorify God in their whole life.[20]

The vision of what might be shapes our ministry in liturgy and our mission in social justice. In the next chapter we will consider how this vision enables us to see some principles of liturgy and social justice.

Shared Pain And Commitment

Still another energy derived from suffering is the manner in which letting pain be pain links us with others. All social movements and organization were born of pain. Not privatized pain or pain kept to oneself or the wallowing in one's own pain, but pain shared. Unemployment shared. Unjust taxes shared. The evil, bitter taste and experiences of racism, of sexism, of ageism—all shared.

Matthew Fox[19]

3. Principles of Liturgy and Social Justice

As the churches of Central and South America have taught us and as the Christian feminists are emphasizing, the relationship between liturgical celebration and the practice of justice is probably the most significant and certainly one of the most urgent questions calling for liturgists' attention today. If there is any dimension of the liturgy which promises to alter our practice and transform our identity as a celebration people, it is this.

John Egan[1]

What has liturgy to do with social justice? Consider these illustrations:

- In South Africa, a young black couple defies the apartheid policies of the government and brings their infant daughter to a church for baptism. There, in the company of an assembly of all races, the child is baptized into the body of Christ.

- In North America, a young child stands beside her parents before the altar. She reaches out her hand as the pastor passes distributing the bread, and says to him: "Christ for me." The pastor smiles and shakes his head, "No, not for you, Sweetheart."

- In Central America, an outspoken, critical archbishop is marked for assassination by his opponents. On a morning in March 1980, as the archbishop, in eucharistic vestments, presides at mass, a sniper aims and shoots. The archbishop, slain, falls to the floor. His prophetic voice is silenced.

- In Europe, a male presider is assisted by a young woman at the altar. A woman and a ten year old girl proclaim the lessons. A young man seated in a wheelchair assists in serving the sacrament to the assembled people.

- In the Soviet Union, a small gathering of Christians

meets for prayer in a home. Their church building, turned first into a museum, has now been destroyed. Officially, their government says there is no God; but there they gather to pray and break bread.

- In Asia, a community gathers for worship. In the course of their liturgy, they employ a small organ imported from North America, sing hymns composed in England, break wafer bread imported from Scandinavia, and share grape wine from France.

- The preacher includes in her sermon examples of stewardship of the environment, care for the wonder and beauty of God's creation. As if to illustrate her homily, her vestments are hand-woven yet simple. Near her at the altar, beeswax feeds the flame of candles; upon the floor rests a vase containing a sheaf of wheat.

- After the liturgy has begun, an elderly native woman enters the church. Though a stranger, she has come to join this community in prayer and worship. The ministers of hospitality who greet her at the door look around uncomfortably, unsure, before finally seating her in a pew near the back.

- In Latin America, a bishop meets with a group of people. In every case, the people are employed by the police and, in fact, are involved in the torture of people confined to prison. In a quiet but stern manner the bishop pastorally advises the people that they will not be allowed to share in the eucharist until they cease their involvement with torture, repent and seek God's forgiveness.

- The prayers of the people are offered by a deacon. In them, prayers are included for peace, for those among the community who are poor and for those who are ill, unable to be present. After the liturgy, a group of people gather in the parish hall to write letters to their members of parliament. Another group moves to the kitchen to prepare a hot noon meal to serve to the area "street people." Yet another small group is blessed and sent away with the sacrament to visit the sick and shut-in who were unable to be present.

- In Ethiopia, the Ethiopian Evangelical Church Mekane Yesus gathers for worship. They worship in a context of severe government persecution and oppression, for the authorities are hostile to the Church's message of hope, faith, justice and peace. In the face of such hos-

Pius X taught us that the liturgy is the indispensable source of the Christian spirit;

Pius XI taught us the authentic Christian spirit is indispensable for social regeneration;

Hence the liturgy is the indispensable source of Christian social regeneration.

Virgil Michel[2]

To the extent liturgy is unconnected with daily life it leads us either to a premature withdrawal from this world as beyond hope or to passive accommodation which confines love, peace and justice to church gatherings, but allows them no role in public life, in work, in economics, politics or culture.

John Egan[3]

24

Social activists who see in the liturgy only a source of personal strength unrelated to their striving for justice, or who abandon the liturgy of the church altogether as an irrelevance, effectively disassociate their social and political activities from the larger plan and purpose of God which the liturgy is intended to recall and to realize.

John Egan[4]

The public dimension of worship is: (a) an occasion where the hope of overcoming barriers, oppression, inequalities and discrimination in society is realized in an anticipatory way; (b) the proclamation of the Kingdom of God as a challenge to secular powers who command complete submission; (c) the eschatological hope celebrated and proclaimed in worship as exposing all human hopes and ideological promises to be penultimate; (d) the equipping of people through worship for their every-day service as a realization of the gift of baptism in daily Christian obedience.

A Lutheran Agenda for Worship[5]

tility and subjugation, the Mekane Yesus Church is growing at a rate of 10 to 15 percent annually.

What has worship to do with social justice? Plenty!

These illustrations highlight several aspects that connect worship with social justice. Note that they relate to justice both within and beyond the worshiping community. They offer contemporary evidence of ancient patterns. Already in Paul's first letter to the Corinthians, we read a critique of worship practice that does not heed *internal* justice within the community:

But in the following instructions I do not commend you. . . . For, in the first place, when you assemble as a church, I hear that there are divisions among you . . . for in eating, each one goes ahead with his own meal, and one is hungry and another is drunk. . . . Do you despise the church of God and humiliate those who have nothing? . . . For any one who eats and drinks without discerning the body eats and drinks judgment upon himself (1 Corinthians 11:17–22, 29).

A critique of worship that is too introspective, devoid of concern for justice in daily lives beyond the walls of the sanctuary, that is, devoid of concern for *external* justice, is forcefully declared by Amos:

I hate, I despise your feasts,
and I take no delight in your solemn assemblies.
Even though you offer me
your burnt offerings and cereal offerings,
I will not accept them,
and the peace offerings of your fatted beasts
I will not look upon.
Take away from me the noise of your songs;
to the melody of your harps I will not listen.
But let justice roll down like waters,
and righteousness like an everflowing stream.

(Amos 5:21–24)

Paul and Amos are but two examples who remind us that from stone altar to temple, from synagogue to house church, from basilica to cathedral, from camp meeting to base community, worship and social justice are intimately and intrinsically linked as a theme that runs through the scriptures, that is brought to expression throughout the Church's history, and that finds contemporary expression in our Sunday morning liturgy. This theme will emerge in subsequent sections of this primer. At this point, however, several general principles relating worship to social justice will be stated.

General Principles of Liturgy and Social Justice

When We Worship We Proclaim That Only God is God

To proclaim God as God is to expose, reveal and challenge the many false gods and idols that vie for our loyalty or attention or which make claims for our allegiance. Such idols include a military system which calls us to put our ultimate trust in weapons; money, which seeks to become our prime concern; status, which wishes to be our principal pursuit; grades, if they are our main motivation for learning, or . . . You can add to the list. Such idols are every bit as real as the molten gods condemned by Isaiah, or the golden calf built in the wilderness.

In worship we proclaim that all other relationships, whether to nation or ruler, class or race, economic or social status, must be secondary to our relationship with God. This principle is summarized in the first commandment: "I am the Lord your God, who brought you out of the land of Egypt, out of the house of bondage. You shall have no other gods before me." In worship our idolatries are confronted and exposed as we remember and celebrate our covenant relationship with the one true God.

To confront and expose our idolatries, however, is not a once-for-all event. It requires an ongoing recentering of ourselves around God's word. The Third Reich in Germany may serve as an example. As the state increased in power, it took on the symbols and trappings of a religion. In that context, the Confessing Church in Germany called upon itself, as well as the state, to recenter itself around the gospel of Jesus Christ. A similar example may be observed in South Africa today. Elements of the church, in issuing *The Kairos Document,*[7] have called the church and state away from an idolatry and toward a prophetic reunderstanding of God's word. Idolatries are always around, seeking to seduce us. Our liturgy exposes those idolatries and proclaims only God as God.

One form of idolatry from which Christians have not always escaped is to image God too narrowly. In particular, we often express a limited and limiting notion of God through the use of images, names and pronouns that are largely if not exclusively masculine in nature. Today we are beginning to realize that though no human speech is adequate to express the mystery and nature of God, we should make every effort to use language that reflects the many facets of God revealed in scripture and in the experience of the people of God.

We Proclaim in Our Liturgy That God is the Creator

When we worship the creator, we declare ourselves to be God's creatures, a part of God's creation. Our awareness and use of God's creation should therefore be respectful and con-

The sheer abundance and diversity of images of God in the Bible bears witness to the futility of focusing on any one image as the ultimate exemplification of God. Unfortunately, the church has done just that. By claiming the male experience to be normative for faith, and by naming the deity as male, we have overemphasized strength and aggressiveness and denied—indeed, repressed—many expressions of faith that focus on God's self-giving, self-emptying love. It would be difficult to say whether our culture's stress on aggressiveness grew out of an overemphasis on God's power and might or whether the images of God's power and might emerged from a society that valued such strength. Regardless, our faith is the poorer for this lopsided view.

True inclusiveness means more than changing words; it means exploring images of God based upon the experience of oppressed peoples. In our context, that means exploring the rich possibilities of feminine imagery, as well as drawing on liturgy and song written by, and in response to, black Americans, Native Peoples, immigrants, and peoples of the Third World. For the sake of justice, and for an accurate representation of God's self-giving, such imagery is essential.

Pamela Payne Allen[6]

Making changes in the concept of the maleness of God and thus the language referring to God is one area where the process and pace of change needs to be slow and careful. A person's concept of God is at the core of his or her spirituality. Authentic change happens best through personal and group reflection, study, experience and celebration. All members of a worshiping community may not be able to embrace changes in language even when there is a careful process. Ways to respect this plurality must be found with neither one group holding the rest back with the "club" of tradition or another group waving the "flag" of enlightenment while leaving the rest bewildered.

The Authors

God the Creator

We give thanks to you . . . for the goodness and love you have made known to us in creation.[8]

It is right to give you thanks and praise . . . sustainer of the universe, you are worthy of glory and praise.

At your command all things came to be: the vast expanse of interstellar space, galaxies, suns, the planets in their courses, and this fragile earth, our island home; by your will they were created and have their being.

From the primal elements you brought forth the human race, and blessed us with memory, reason, and skill; you made us the stewards of creation.[9]

You have filled all creation with light and life; heaven and earth are full of your glory.[10]

We do give thanks to you . . . for the gifts of creation and life. You divided the light from the darkness and the water from the dry land; you made us in the image of yourself, and breathed into us the breath of life.[11]

All things are of your making all times and seasons obey your laws, but you chose to create [us] in your own image, setting [us] over the whole world in all its wonder. You made [us] the steward of creation, to praise you day by day, for the marvels of your wisdom and power.[12]

It is indeed right that we should praise you, gracious God, for you created all things. You formed us in your own image, male and female you created us.[13]

Holy God, source of life and goodness, all creation rightly gives you praise. In the fullness of time, you sent your Son Jesus Christ, to share our human nature, to live and die as one of us, to reconcile us to you. . . .

He healed the sick and ate and drank with outcasts and sinners; he opened the eyes of the blind and proclaimed the good news of your kingdom to the poor and to those in need. In all things he fulfilled your gracious will.[14]

---

serving; our relationship within the creation should be harmonious. The account of creation in Genesis reminds humankind that we are placed within the created order as stewards, not exploiters.

The four ancient elements of the universe—earth, air, fire and water—are present within our worship. Elements of creation are thus integral to our worship experience: water, fire, ashes, bread, wine, incense, beeswax, wood, stone, wool, linen, and, most especially, human beings. The list could go on and on. These elements of creation are used by God and by the worship assembly to communicate God's, the creator's, presence. Such affirmation of the creation within worship underscores God's continuing blessing of creation; God's resounding "It is good!" echoes through the ages. Such an affirmation of the created order should encourage the worship assembly to make authentic use of the creation in worship: real flowers, not plastic; genuine and rich fabric, not synthetic materials; fire, not flickering light bulbs.

In Our Liturgy We Commemorate and Celebrate the Death and Resurrection of Jesus Christ

The assembly gathers for worship on the day of the Lord's

resurrection. The entire church year builds from Advent, Christmas and Epiphany through Lent toward the annual remembrance of Christ's death and resurrection. The fifty days of Easter derive from that annual remembrance and move us toward the gift of the Spirit at Pentecost. In weekly cycles commemorating Christ's resurrection we move through a church year centered upon the death and new life of Christ.

Christ's exodus from death to new life is a victory over death, a liberation from slavery to sin. It is a liberation in which we share because of our baptism into Christ's death and resurrection. As God's action in the exodus was a liberation from slavery, so in God's action of raising Christ from death to life there is a liberation from all kinds of deadly slavery. Baptized into this covenantal relationship, we pledge ourselves to seek the liberation of others from all kinds of slavery and death. Our baptismal covenant links us in a vertical relationship with God and within a horizontal relationship embracing the whole human family.

In Worship We Celebrate the Incarnation and Continued Presence of Jesus Christ

To tell the stories of Jesus' life and ministry is to remember his incarnation into a specific time and place and also communicate social justice themes. Jesus was born in an occupied land, was homeless at birth, a refugee early in his life. He was from among the poor of the land. Yet Jesus the Christ has promised to be with us always. In his presence today, Jesus himself relates to, and thus joins us to, people of our own time who are poor and outcast. Jesus lived and moved among the marginalized: the bleeding woman who reached out to him from the dusty street, Zacchaeus in the tree, the adulterous woman, tax collectors, a Samaritan woman seeking water. Jesus lives and moves among the marginalized still. We are called to share in these relationships and the consequent responsibilities. Is it any wonder that the Roman Catholic Latin American bishops' conferences at Medellín in 1968, and Puebla in 1979, pleaded for the church to have a preferential option for the poor?

In Our Liturgy We Invoke the Presence and Action of the Transforming Holy Spirit

Jesus gifted the church with the Spirit. In our worship we pray to God through Jesus Christ, in the Holy Spirit. This Spirit has called and gathered us into relationship with God and with one another. The sanctifying grace of the Holy Spirit is thus not primarily a privatistic, pietistic, other-worldly influence, but rather transforms and gifts us to continue the ministry of Jesus Christ in the world today. It is the Spirit that calls us toward a unity among all women and men within the body of Christ.

The Death and Resurrection of Jesus

*By the power of the Holy Spirit
he took flesh of the Virgin Mary
and shared our human nature.
He lived and died as one of us,
to reconcile us to you. . . .*

*In fulfillment of your will
he stretched out his hands in suffering,
to bring release to those who place their hope
   in you;
and so he won for you a holy people.*

*He chose to bear our griefs and sorrows,
and to give up his life on the cross,
that he might shatter the chains of evil and
   death,
and banish the darkness of sin and despair.
By his resurrection
he brings us into the light of your presence.*

*Now with all creation we raise our voices
to proclaim the glory of your name.*[15]

*We give you thanks and praise . . .
because in sending Jesus, your Son, to us
you showed us how much you love us.
He cares for the poor and the hungry.
He suffers with the sick and the rejected.*

*Betrayed and forsaken, he did not strike back
but overcame hatred with love.
On the cross
he defeated the power of sin and death.
By raising him from the dead
you show us the power of your love
to bring new life to all your people.*[16]

The Incarnation

*. . . you so loved the world
that in the fullness of time
you sent your only Son to be our Savior.
He was conceived through the power of the
    Holy Spirit,
and born of the Virgin Mary,
[one] like us in all things but sin.*

*To the poor he proclaimed the good news of
    salvation,
to prisoners, freedom,
and to those in sorrow, joy.
In fulfillment of your will
he gave himself up to death;
but by rising from the dead,
he destroyed death and restored life.*

*And that we might live
no longer for ourselves but for him,
he sent the Holy Spirit from you . . .
as his first gift to those who believe,
to complete his work on earth
and bring us the fullness of grace.*[17]

The Transforming Spirit

*We praise and thank you through Jesus
    Christ our Lord
for your presence and action in the world.
In the midst of conflict and division,
we know it is you
who turn our minds to thoughts of peace.*

*Your Spirit changes our hearts:
enemies begin to speak to one another,
those who were estranged join hands in
    friendship,
and nations seek the way of peace together.
Your Spirit is at work
when understanding puts an end to strife,
when hatred is quenched by mercy,
and vengeance gives way to forgiveness.*[18]

Liturgy has the potential to become a powerful means of conscientization, but if it is seen solely as that, we shall once again have distorted it, if not destroyed it.

John Egan[19]

Many see the work of the Holy Spirit in the process of liturgical renewal and the integration of liturgy and social justice. One example of the Spirit's sanctifying presence may be found in Mexico where a cathedral and a people were transformed. The cathedral in Cuernavaca was an ornate structure. As a parish, it was among the first to be touched by the wave of liturgical renewal in the Roman Catholic Church. It may be hard to imagine an elaborate cathedral and liturgical renewal as elements of a revolutionary transformation. Yet these were the means by which the bishop of Cuernavaca was able to "hear the cry of the poor" in his diocese. With the assistance of the monks at a nearby Benedictine Abbey, the bishop initiated changes in the decor of the cathedral. Golden images were removed. As the walls were being stripped of their finery, ancient murals of the indigenous people were uncovered. The distance between the people and the presider was lessened, the altar and presider were turned so as to face the people. As other liturgical changes took place, more poor people began to feel that this, too, was their church. Bishop Mendez-Arceo began to meet and listen to these people, their hardships and their hopes. As he listened, he as well as the cathedral was transformed. He and many priests and sisters began to rethink their roles. Strong leaders emerged from among the people. They gathered in small groups to pray, listen to the word, reflect—and to act. This brought the people, the bishop and church workers into many situations of conflict with those who were quite content for poor people to remain voiceless and powerless.

In Our Liturgy, We Proclaim and Model the Kingdom, or Reign of God

That is, we "play," rehearse and experience a foretaste of the reign of God within the worshiping assembly. Thereby we are both challenged and enabled to proclaim and model this reign in our weekday living. Divisions that are known in society are—*or should be*—banished within our worship assembly. Racism, sexism, ageism, ideologies and political dogma are challenged by God's reign. We are called to put them aside in our worship and accept a new identity, as equal members in the body of Christ. By virtue of our baptism we are neither Jew nor Greek, slave nor free, male nor female, black nor white, but all one in Christ. In the world beyond our worship there is hunger; but inside the worshiping assembly all are fed equally from God's gracious table as a sign of how life might be ordered. In the world beyond our worship there is war and hostility; but inside the worshiping assembly all share the peace of the Lord as a sign of how life might be lived. In the world beyond our worship there is hostility and suspicion toward the stranger; but inside the worshiping community the stranger is hospitably welcomed. In the world beyond our worship death reigns with seeming impunity; but inside the liturgical gathering, death is overcome and we celebrate life in spite of death.

In Worship We Ritually Express Our Longings for an Alternative Future

Our longing to be whole, forgiven and to belong is brought to our worship and to occasions to remember or reaffirm our baptismal covenant. Our longing for God's *shalom,* for peace and justice, for an end to war and oppression, for all the world to be fed, is brought to expression in our prayers, addressed to God, but affirmed by the whole assembly with its "Amen." Our longing to be a part of community is brought to the fellowship of the assembly. Our longing to extend the church's mission, to serve those in any need, is brought to the offerings where we offer ourselves, our time and talents, our bread, wine and money, as symbols of who we are.

But those longings are not left within the sanctuary. Those very longings which come to ritual expression in liturgy become an agenda, a mandate for our daily lives. In the ritual expression, these longings shape us, form our identity, make us who we are as people of God. We bear that identity into all the world as instruments of God's peace, as "little Christs" called and sent not only to proclaim God's reign, but to live it.

Our Liturgy Sustains and Nourishes Us in Our Ministries as Disciples of Jesus Christ

Our practice of the "lifestyle of the kingdom" on Sunday prepares us to live these attributes of the reign of God in our everyday, weekday lives, in our work and within our relationships. In gathering together around word, baptism and eucharist, we recenter ourselves and remind ourselves who and whose we are. We bring to our worship the wounds and sorrows encountered during the week and find comfort, healing, forgiveness and consolation in God's word. We also find the vision and strength to return to the world to live as Christ's disciples, as instruments of God's peace. Our worship is thus an occasion and source of hope, encouragement and joy, shared among the people of God.

As an example, consider a community of women in Calcutta. Gathered around a modern saint, these sisters of Mother Teresa together seek to embody the presence of Christ amidst a scene of almost unimaginable poverty, hunger, sorrow and death. Their ministry includes orphanages for abandoned children, houses of refuge for hungry people and hospices for the dying. It is the ministry of some sisters among them to begin the day by gathering the infants born and abandoned on the streets during the night. Some of the infants are rescued and placed in orphanages. Other babies are simply held by warm, loving arms until they die. This community of sisters begins each and every day of such ministry with scripture,

---

In every generation some people are called by name consciously to serve this Kingdom and its justice as revealed in Jesus. They are called Christians, and together, as a new humanity, they have the unenviable responsibility of representing the hope of a higher justice and working for its realization.

Mark Searle[20]

God's justice is done when arbitration is transformed by reconciliation; when people become more than objects of desire, manipulation, and profit; when poverty is confronted by asking, not how much the poor require, but how much the rich need; when the goods of the earth are looked upon, not as sources of private profit, but as sacraments of divine and human intercommunication. As and when such things occur, however rarely or fleetingly, then God's justice is done, and there the rule or Kingdom of God becomes manifest. For the justice of God that the liturgy proclaims *is* the Kingdom of God.

Mark Searle[21]

As Christians we are convinced that the work we do for justice, no more or less than the liturgical action itself, is *opus dei,* in which we are not independent operators, but fellow workers with Christ and ministers of his Spirit. This must save us from the hubris of success and the despondency of apparent failure, both of which are the fruits of rugged individualism.

John Egan[22]

The celebrated ones will not mind my recalling that the Nazis got simple preachers of the gospel like Pastor Paul Schneider early—he was arrested in 1937, tortured to death at Buchenwald in 1939—while professors like Dietrich Bonhoeffer made it to Hitler's last month and dignitaries like Martin Niemoller escaped with their lives. Much of the most eloquent testimony to us [about the terror of South Africa's State of Emergency] came from pastors and members whose names you will never hear. They are, to remember a phrase, people whose names are written in the Book of Life.

Martin E. Marty[23]

Our Corporate Identity

Source of life and goodness,
you have created all things,
to fill your creatures with every blessing. . . .
You formed the human race in your own
* likeness:*
male and female you created them
and set them over the whole world
to serve you, their creator,
and to rule over all creatures.[24]

The baptized people of God gather for worship in a broken world, a world plagued by hunger, addiction, despair, and alienation; divided by political, economic and racial ideologies; scarred by the Holocaust and other genocides; oppressed by tyranny; wounded by torture and war; and overshadowed by the threatening cloud of nuclear catastrophe. In such a world, Christians gather for worship affirming the wonder and goodness of God's creation, and acknowledging thereby God as creator and sovereign.[25]

prayer and the eucharist. Their worship sustains, nurtures and continues to make possible their ministry and witness.

The Worshiping Assembly Transcends Our Individuality and Emphasizes Our Corporate Identity

The church is defined as the baptized *assembly* gathered around word and sacrament. The emphasis is upon the gathered community. In our worship, the assembly acts. We make corporate confession, articulating the implicit nature of common sin, the systemic nature of evil, the collective responsibility of our actions and of our indifference. We move on with words of assurance that there is occasion for *new* beginnings, for the possibility of corporate conversion and change. The gathered assembly is a weekly reminder that in Christ we are one. Barriers of society are dismantled and washed away at baptism. The norms of society are displaced by the ethics of the kingdom when the assembly gathers.

Next Sunday when you gather with others for worship, look around you with care and compassion upon your sisters and brothers in Christ. But look with a critical eye as well. What do you see? Is there in fact a true gathering of God's people? Or are they mostly all alike: of the same race, of similar economic standing, healthy and whole? Where are the disabled, the retarded? Where are the "street people"? Is your corporate identity a true reflection of the diversity of God's human family or is it a ghetto?

Worship Celebrates Women and Men in Community

The scriptures speak of there being neither male nor female in the body of Christ. Yet, for centuries there has been a flagrant distinction made between men and women in the community of the church. This principle of worship and social justice thus accuses and judges us, for women (and children) are in practice more often than not *unequal.* An awareness of this principle will lead worshiping communities to affirm the full participation of women in worship, to a sensitivity for the need of language that is inclusive of all, and to care in balancing the roles of women and men (and older children) in liturgical ministries.

A growing edge for many church people today is the concern for using words and images which include and embody all of the members of the worshiping community and their experiences. It is vital that people hear and see that they are part of this community. The pain of exclusion or invisibility can disillusion those who experience it and leave the entire community the poorer. It is a hopeful sign that denominational bodies have undertaken formal studies of the role of women in the church and the question of inclusive language. There have been some helpful changes, but there are still many challenges to be studied and addressed.

Language Referring to the Worshiping Community

Terms such as man, mankind, forefathers, family of man, and certain uses of he, his and him once were generic terms which could be used to include both men and women. Because these terms are in fact often used to refer only to males, their use has become ambiguous and increasingly is perceived to exclude women. Wherever possible, these terms should not be used. They can often easily be replaced with other words which may in fact be more faithful to the original text. (It is to be noted that the term "man," as it is employed in many biblical and liturgical texts, is used to translate *adam, anthropos* or *homo,* words which actually mean "human" rather than "male.") Expressions such as the following may be used to designate individuals or groups:
brothers and sisters, sons and daughters, men and women, humanity, human race, humankind, people(s), companion, family, friends, faithful, children, all/we/us, whole world, church, community, ancestors, he/she, forerunners.

However, simple substitution is not always theologically or linguistically appropriate and entire passages sometimes need to be rewritten. Using a plural pronoun instead of a singular, or using the passive voice can be another way to deal with difficult terms or phrasing.

Language and Prayers Addressing the Worshiping Community

If women form part of the worshiping community, formal greetings such as "sisters and brothers," "friends," or other phrases should be used. Those preaching or leading prayers should be sensitive to the phrases they use so that the full participation of women is upheld.

Language Referring to Women

Some liturgical texts imply the inferiority of women and their natural subjection to men. These texts generally are biblical or biblically inspired and reflect the culture in which they were composed, or culturally conditioned theological argumentation. An example would be the subjection of wives to husbands indicated in Ephesians 5 and Colossians 3. The problems that arise from such texts may in some cases be relieved by more careful translation. Another possible solution is careful explanation of the texts. In other cases particular verses or entire pericopes may have to be deleted from liturgical use, and there is ample precedent for such selectivity. Each passage requires individual study and judgment regarding the approach that is to be taken.

International Commission on English in the Liturgy[26]

Our Liturgy Affirms and Interacts With Its Cultural Setting

Worship is linked to its scriptural roots in the life and ministry of Jesus of Nazareth. But each generation and each local church is challenged to faithfully relate that scriptural origin to its own context, and to make worship faithfully indigenous in its cultural setting. Inevitably, this raises difficult questions. For example, at the World Council of Churches General Assembly in 1983, some delegates from the South Pacific islands asked whether coconuts and rice wine could be used as the elements in their eucharist, since wheat bread and grape wine were alien to their cultural context. What is the faithful response to such a question?

To be aware of one's cultural setting involves one in an examination of the totality of worship: texts, architecture, vestments, music, instruments and so on. Consider the example of northern Canada. If you had been present at a Bible class in northern Labrador in the early part of this century, you would have heard a missionary teaching about Christ as the "harp seal pup of God" instead of the "lamb of God." The native people of that area had never seen a sheep, and Dr. Wilfred Grenfell felt that the harp seal pup more adequately

32

Prayers For The Church Around The World

Remember the Church in Brazil, and praise God for the courageous struggles of many for justice and human dignity for all people, especially the poor.

Remember the Church in Namibia and Zimbabwe, and praise God that [Christians] there are seeking to make their contribution to the process of nation-building.

Remember the Church in Argentina, and praise God for those who have been martyred for their witness to God's option for the oppressed, the poor, the forgotten.

Remember the Church in South Africa, Botswana, Lesotho, and Swaziland, and praise God for all who with courage and fortitude are bearing witness to Christ as partisans of the oppressed and reconcilers of the divided.

Remember the Church in Sri Lanka, Madagascar, and the other independent countries and islands of the Indian Ocean, and praise God for all those who seek the reconciliation of tensions between ethnic groups.

Preparing By Prayer[27]

bore the biblical connotations for these people. Or, if you had been present at the Palm Sunday worship for a community of Dene in Fort Simpson in 1982, you would have held a pine bough in your hand during the procession instead of a palm branch. You would have observed that the presiding minister's vestments were adorned with moose hair and porcupine quills. You would have felt the drums pulsing with your own heart beat as you listened to the Dene sing in their own chanting, wailing song.

The heart cries out in prayer, song and images shaped by one's culture, race and experience. Some congregations are unicultural while others are multicultural. Some are unilingual while others use a multitude of languages in their worship. Whatever your congregational reality, it is helpful to be aware of the role which culture plays in liturgical expression. Facilitating cross-cultural understanding through the prism of liturgy can be a community-building experience.

If yours is a multicultural congregation, you might consider ways to celebrate different cultures that are authentic and integral to the liturgy, and not merely token or inappropriate. This could be through song, prayer, liturgical dance or procession. Banners, altar cloths, vessels for the eucharist, or art forms such as carvings, sculptures or stations of the cross could be used. Invite people who are new citizens, whether by choice or through exile, to participate in the visible ministries exercised during the liturgy. For example, in one large, urban parish, each cultural grouping represented within the congregation has been asked to plan a special Sunday liturgy. Afterward, people are invited to taste ethnic foods, enjoy dance, music and other art forms in order to learn about the country and experiences of the group.

At the Same Time, Worship Critiques Its Cultural Setting

This principle is related to those described above that proclaim God as God in exposing idols and that rehearse the values and lifestyle of God's reign. As no culture is perfectly consistent with the gospel, there are idols and values in every culture that worship needs to expose and challenge. In addition, while being sensitive to the different ethnic cultures represented in any of our congregations, it is also crucial to be aware of a larger, more dominant context within which many of the other cultures exist. Various names have been used to describe ours: consumer culture and western culture are two.

Current bumper stickers, only partly in jest, declare: "This car stops at all garage sales" or that human beings are "Born to shop." Critically examined, these statements lay bare the idolatry of this consumer culture.

What values give birth to such a statement? Without exploring in depth here, we can see that the ways in which Jesus interacted with people affirms a higher calling than being "born to shop." As well, the reign of God promises more than the winning of a lottery. Some elements of the church glibly proclaim that you can accept Jesus into your heart and then expect to have follow wealth, happiness, fame and fortune. The liturgy of the church says otherwise. In our worship, we are called to insure that the values and symbols of the consumer kingdom do not shrewdly and deceitfully displace the values and symbols of the reign of God.

In Worship We Express an Awareness of Historical and Global Realities

That is to say, we worship in a given time and space, and like Jesus' time ours is laden with social justice realities. Historically, we worship in the era of Auschwitz and Hiroshima, twin holocausts that have indelibly scarred us and raised implications for us in how we worship. The ancient Greeks had two words for time: *chronos* was the normal, chronological unfolding of history; *kairos* described the sacred, holy moments of history. We worship as people of God sensitive to and aware of the "kairos" moments within the "chronos" of our lives. In other words, we worship with a keen sense of memory but also with the anticipation of God's reign. This keen sense of memory is attentive to "the underside of history," the history of the victims which has usually been overlooked by the victors who write the official histories. In our worship we celebrate already the presence of God's reign even as we await its final consummation. Our global awareness in worship begins in our local setting and extends outward through city, province, nation, continent and planet. Issues and events are addressed by God's word, are incorporated into our prayers and are shaped into our lives and our longings.

A good example of worship with such an awareness may

A "Gospel" is a book of revelation, an ultimate source or reference wherein we find ourselves revealed. A gospel is a response to the questions of who we are, what we may hope for, how we may aspire to act, what endures, what is important, what is of true value. A gospel, then, is an expression of who or what is our functional god.

We will inevitably be confronted with at least two competing gospels or books of revelation in American society. These gospels differ as radically as light and darkness, life and death, freedom and slavery, fidelity and unfaithfulness. . . . These competing life-forms can be expressed as the "gospels of Personhood and Commodity: the Person Form and the Commodity Form; the Person-god and the Thing-god. Each has its own "church," you might say, its own cults and liturgical rites, its own special language, and its own concept of the heretical.

One form of life, one gospel, reveals men and women as replaceable and marketable commodities; another gospel, inalterably opposed to the first, reveals persons as irreplaceable and uniquely free beings. Some people having formal membership in a Christian church may in reality follow the gospel of the culture, and belong to the secular church of "the thing." Others, not formally belonging to a Christian church or to a synagogue, may actually be giving their life-commitments to the message and truth revealed in the covenantal Lord of the Jewish Bible or in Jesus Christ as true God and True human person.

John Kavanagh[28]

34

A Creed from South Africa

Jesus has taught us to speak of hope as the coming of God's Kingdom.

We believe that God is at work in our world turning hopeless and evil situations into good.

We believe that goodness and justice and love will triumph in the end, and that tyranny and oppression cannot last forever.

One day 'all tears will be wiped away' and 'the lamb will lie down with the lion.'

True peace and true reconciliation are not only desirable, they are assured and guaranteed.

This is our faith, and our hope.[29]

be observed, perhaps surprisingly, at monasteries. Virgil Michel and Thomas Merton and their monastic communities could be mentioned, but consider rather Taizé, a small, ecumenical monastic community located in the beautiful, pastoral countryside of southern France. High above the green fields of Burgundy, intersecting contrails of Mirage jet fighters dispute the notion that Taizé is remote and isolated. Since 1940, an ecumenical community of brothers has gathered and grown near the small village of Taizé. During World War II, Taizé was a haven for Jews escaping the death camps of the Third Reich. Now it is a place of pilgrimage for young people from all over the world. Three times a day the brothers and their guests gather in the Church of Reconciliation for scripture reading, song, silence and prayer. Praise and thanksgiving, intercession and lament give shape and content to their communal prayer. At the same time in other parts of the world, "cell groups" of three Taizé brothers gather thrice daily for prayer. Their locales are not as idyllic as Taizé, for they seek out the poorest places on earth to name as home: Hell's Kitchen in Manhattan, Haiti and Calcutta are among them. But whether in Burgundy or Haiti, their prayer is shaped and informed by an awareness of the poverty, oppression, sorrow and tragedy of humanity's inhumanity. Their prayer and their lives of ministry are turned toward the hope and shalom of God's reign.

These principles summarize some of the connections between worship and social justice. In the following sections on Gathering, Word, Baptism, Eucharist and Sending Forth, they will be amplified and expanded.

4. The Gathering of God's People

Introduction

The Gathering and Social Justice

The People Who Worship
We gather because we are called
Our gathering emphasizes community
Our gathering is an experience of radical equality
In our gathering children are hospitably welcomed
Our gathering is characterized by joy and hope

The God We Worship
Our gathering names God as true God
Gathering on Sunday proclaims the sovereignty and presence of the risen Christ
Our Sunday gathering affirms the values of the sabbath

Our Mission and Ministry
In our gathering we show care for one another
In our gathering the many different gifts are brought together into unity
In our gathering we acknowledge that we are sinners

The Liturgical Celebration

Non-Verbal Dimensions
Hospitality
Architecture

Verbal Dimensions
Song
Greeting
Confession and reminder of baptism
Prayer

Blessed are you, gracious God,
creator of heaven and earth;
we give you thanks and praise
through Jesus Christ our Lord,
who on this first day of the week
overcame death and the grave,
and by his glorious resurrection
opened to us the way of everlasting life.
In our unending joy
we echo on earth the song of the angels in
* heaven*
as we raise our voices
to proclaim the glory of your name.[1]

. . . Rhythm . . . makes things memorable,
as in music, poetry, rhetoric, architecture,
and the plastic arts no less than in liturgical
worship. Rhythm constantly insinuates, as
propagandists know. It constantly reasserts,
as good teachers know. It constantly forms
individuals into units, as demagogues and
cheerleaders know. It both shrouds and
bares meaning which escapes mere words, as
poets know. It fuses people to their values
and forges them to common purpose, as ora-
tors such as Cato, Churchill, and Martin
Luther King knew. It frees from sound and
offers vision for those who yearn for it, as
the preacher of the Sermon on the Mount
knew. Liturgical ministers who are irrepara-
bly arhythmic should be restrained from
ministering in the liturgy.

Aidan Kavanagh[2]

In the first part of our Sunday liturgy—what we are calling "the gathering of God's people," or the liturgy of gathering—we simply come together: we gather.

Much of the gathering liturgy is non-verbal, informal and somewhat spontaneous; the community's worship begins long before the presiding minister enters and before the printed service in the bulletin or worship-book begins. Thus the many members of the worshiping community first of all simply come together physically and socially in the place of worship. They come alone or as families, a few at first, then many together. They arrive in different moods and states of expectation, from a variety of weekday experiences, and with diverse needs.

The gathering people take their places in a particular environment. This consists in part of the architectural features of the church building, and in part of the interpersonal relationships that exist among the assembled people.

The formal, structured and more verbal phase of the gathering liturgy begins when the presiding minister (perhaps with other ministers and choir) enters. The manner in which Christian communities formally gather varies. Some call this "The Entrance Rite," others "The Approach" or other terms. In some traditions the gathering rite is fairly brief, in others more extended. It may include processions of people, liturgical dance, banners, cross and candle, incense, or the sprinkling of people with water in remembrance of their baptism. Whatever it is termed, however it is done, verbal and non-verbal, it generally includes everything up to the proclamation of the word of God.

Most commonly, the formal part of the gathering liturgy includes an opening song (hymn), and perhaps other singing; a scripture sentence, apostolic greeting, or sign of the cross, plus a more informal and personal greeting by the presider; a prayer of confession, remembrance of baptism, or both; and a short prayer.

What Is Your Own Experience?

What do you really like and what really bothers you about the way you and the rest of your congregation actually come together for Sunday worship?

Imagine yourself to be a stranger coming to worship with your congregation. What would be your first impressions?

. . . it is right that we should give you thanks and glory:
you alone are God, living and true.

Through all eternity you live in unapproachable light.
Source of life and goodness, you have created all things,
to fill your creatures with every blessing and lead all [people] to the joyful vision of your light.[3]

. . . hear the prayers of the family you have gathered here before you.
In mercy and love unite all your children wherever they may be.[4]

The Gathering and Social Justice

Does the liturgy of gathering have any meaning and significance aside from the purely practical one of getting everybody in their places before Sunday worship begins? And if there is some deeper purpose, then how, if at all, is it relevant to social justice? How might it promote social justice values?

In fact, the wisdom of the Christian tradition—based on the gospel of Jesus Christ, the living tradition of the church through the ages, the best of the church's experience of worship—tells us that the gathering liturgy has a very profound meaning. It also sets before us a vision of the gathering liturgy that demonstrates a clear and instrinsic relationship between this part of our Sunday liturgy and social justice.

The liturgy of gathering speaks of the people who worship, the God we worship, and our mission and ministry.

The People Who Worship

We Gather Because We Are Called

In rhythms of weeks, seasons and festivals the people of God gather to worship our God. We gather as baptized children of God, sisters and brothers of Jesus Christ and of one another, all members of the church. We come together also as followers and disciples of Jesus Christ, gifted for ministry by the Holy Spirit, carrying out the mission of the church.

We gather to worship by God's command at Sinai, by Jesus' command to give thanks in his remembrance until his return. We gather by Jesus' invitation and in his presence. We gather to join our individual life stories with our common community story and together to blend them with Christ's story—*the* story of God in Christ loving humanity. We gather in response to God's Spirit who calls, enlightens and sanctifies us. We gather to find meaning for ourselves, to encounter God in worship, to offer God our creator our prayer, praise and thanksgiving. We gather to seek forgiveness, to be transformed into new persons enabled to live new lives in Christ and the

Presiding Minister. We use the terms *presiding minister, presider,* or *the minister* interchangeably for the ordained person who presides at the Sunday liturgy. Other ministers, whether ordained or lay, will be termed *assisting ministers.*

The Authors

Assembly. Modern liturgists use the term *assembly* to include all those who are worshiping. In contrast, *congregation* refers to those without special ministerial roles; often, the laity as opposed to the clergy. Outside the liturgy, of course, *congregation* may be used to refer to the entire local church community or parish.

The Authors

Each denomination and congregation has different ways of involving (and not involving) and integrating (or excluding) children in the worship experience. Some basic points to consider are the following.

Music. Are the children taught to sing the music which the community uses? Are there some songs or hymns which are easier for children to sing? Children's choirs can be viewed as a vital ministry to the worshiping community or as a cute group of performers.

Sunday School. If the children leave the service at some point for Sunday school, are they formally welcomed back or do they skip back to their seats virtually unnoticed? Is there an opportunity for them to share what they learned or did?

Ministry. An ideal place for children to observe and learn the practice of charity and justice is in the worshiping community (complemented by the home, of course). Gradually involving children in ministries is one way to do this. Another is to frequently refer to children's needs throughout the world and within the community. This could be voiced through prayer or song or through art-forms.

Equality. If the worshiping community prays the "Our Father" or another prayer regularly, the entire community could hold hands while it is prayed. This is one tangible sign to the children that they belong. When sharing a "sign of peace," children too enjoy being recognized and joining in.

The Authors

Holy Spirit. We gather to pray to God our lament and sorrow, our intercessions and needs, confident of God's mercy and grace. We gather in hospitable assembly with guests, onlookers, those who are exploring whether or not to join the journey of the baptized community. We gather as witnesses to good news ready to be strengthened, sustained, encouraged and empowered to share that good news in everyday living.

Our Gathering Emphasizes Community

In worship there is an emphasis upon people together, a family, a community of equals who deeply care for one another. The community of God's people overwhelms our great diversity, whereas in society those differences often are magnified. Though individuality is respected, each person honored, excessive individualism is addressed and steadfastly challenged by our sense of belonging to a community.

Sometimes a gift from another part of the church can be illuminating. Consider the Xhosa proverb from the church in southern Africa: *Umntu ngumntu ngabantu.* It translates: "A person is a person because of other people." An African Christian would see his/her identity grounded in the community, among the people. A similar sense of corporate identity is to be found within the church in northern Canada, among the Dene. The Dene people speak of a sense of community that transcends time and space. For example, they speak of their land as being held in trust by their generation *from* their ancestors *for* their descendants. The land is not theirs individually, but belongs to the people. Such a community dimension infuses the church of Christ: we are a people—the people of God.

The primary non-verbal symbol or focus in this gathering is thus neither altar nor pulpit, cross nor minister, but the people themselves. It is the assembly that is the focus. For in this gathered people Christ is present among us as we together, collectively, constitute the body of Christ.

Our Gathering Is an Experience of Radical Equality

In the community's worship, the mutual recognition of sisters and brothers in Christ, the essential equality among the baptized is an experience of the reign of God. Recall that many of Jesus' parables of the kingdom have to do with redeemed human relationships, often with the reversal of personal roles. For example, those who seek the position of honor for themselves at the wedding feast, or those who shun their hospitable invitations to the banquet, or Lazarus and the rich man. In worship we "play," model, rehearse and participate in the reign of God. We gather as equals in the eyes of God, as baptized children of God. We are free to graciously welcome and honor one another within the assembly because we have been baptismally welcomed into the reign of God.

In Our Gathering Children Are Hospitably Welcomed

One dimension of worship is sometimes called sacred play, and who can better teach us about this than children? Yet, how often do we plan for and try to learn from the children in our midst? Considering children's needs and contributions is a particular challenge. It is also a unique invitation to growth, fresh insights, and a chance to better understand a familiar saying of Jesus: *Unless you change and become like little children, you cannot enter the kingdom of heaven.*

Some denominations are more practiced in this area than others, and thus this is an excellent area for ecumenical exchange. It is an area which is bound to rattle some long-held beliefs about the role, behavior and place of children. Taking children seriously as persons who have a faith life to be nourished and shared within the community raises deeper theological and doctrinal questions as well. For example, many churches are presently reexamining the question of when children should begin to participate fully in the eucharist. In the Eastern Orthodox Churches, children have regularly been included in the eucharist from the day of their baptism. Not so in the Western Churches, in which children have long been

---

South Africa is one of the few countries in the world which is ruled by a declared Christian government. Christian nationalism is what they subscribe to. According to the former Prime Minister, Vorster, it is an ideology that most closely resembles nazism in Hitler's Germany and fascism in Mussolini's Italy. No-one who has studied the real situation in South Africa with open eyes has reason to doubt the Prime Minister's words. The white minority regime stops at no method to maintain and consolidate its power.

But out of the suffering of the Black People a song is born. The singer can be silenced, but never the song; the hope of a free country, the dream of freedom, this song can never be taken from the people.

It booms out from the court-room where the young people accused of treason sing their freedom-songs with raised fists.

It booms out from Pretoria Central Prison where those condemned to death sing day-in, day-out from their cells. The night before an execution there is never silence, and when dawn breaks the condemned man sings the song of his comrades during the last steps through the double-door to the gallows.

But above all else the South African song is a victory-song, a defiant hymn.

This song sounds out when two thousand women and children gather on a sandy field outside Capetown. They refuse to be separated from their menfolk and sent to Transkei, a "homeland" a thousand miles away, where starvation and sickness awaits them, a reserve that many have never been in, but which is now according to the apartheid policy the only legal domicile for these women. Despite constant harassment from the police, despite the cold and rain the women stand there round the fires and the wooden cross—and sing hymns. After six weeks of unbroken singing the patience of the police ends. Early one morning, just before dawn, they strike. Heavily armed and with dogs they occupy the small hills around the camp. The women gather round the cross, fall to their knees in the wet sand and pray. Then they dance round the cross, the symbol of this folly. These women have lost everything—their homes, their families, their jobs and their possessions. They have nothing more to lose—only their chains, but everything to win. Therefore they are filled with songs of praise. "Happy are you when people hate you, reject you, insult you, and say you are evil, all because of the Son of Man! Be glad when that happens, and dance for joy." The police they don't dance, and why should they? They have everything to lose and nothing to win. "But how terrible for you who are rich now; you have had your easy life! How terrible for you who are full now; you will go hungry! How terrible for you who laugh now; you will mourn and weep!" When the sun slowly rises over the mountain peaks, one of the women begins with "Akanamandla" and in triumph the crowd makes for the police-trucks to let themselves be arrested. "Akanamandla"—He has no power! Halleluya! Satan is powerless!

Anders Nyberg[5]

The Celebration of the Lord's Day

On the day which is called Sun-day, all, whether they live in the town or in the country, gather in the same place.

We hold this meeting of us all on Sunday because it is the first day, the day when God transformed matter and darkness and created the world, and also because it was on this same day that Jesus Christ, our Saviour, rose from the dead.

Justin Martyr[6]

baptized but not welcomed at the eucharistic table until years afterward. Many churches are currently seeking to again affirm baptism as the sacramental means by which people are fully initiated into the eucharistic life of the assembly, regardless of their age.

Let us reflect for a moment on the primary messages a child might receive in an average Sunday worship experience. What can she see? do? hear? sing? Is he shushed, told to sit still, talked down to or ignored? How is she included in the primary elements of worship? Would a child see worship as something to be endured, or as a special family experience? Would a child feel valued as a member of a community, or perceived as someone who causes problems? Is the atmosphere such that she feels welcome to bring her concerns to the prayer of the community?

Our Gathering Is Characterized by Joy and Hope

Confident of Jesus' promise that where two or three are gathered in his name, Christ is present, the assembly joyfully celebrates the presence of Christ. We gather also abounding in hope, for the resurrection of Jesus Christ assures us of a hope, for though we may not know what the future holds, we know who holds the future.

The God We Worship

Our Gathering Names God As True God

In gathering as God's people, the community declares the ultimate sovereignty of God in their lives. It is to God that our ultimate loyalty, allegiance and trust belong. Implicit in that declaration is a challenge to secular powers and authorities who command submission or loyalty. It is this social-justice implication in worship that has moved some witnesses to Christ, such as Polycarp, Dietrich Bonhoeffer, Perpetua and Felicity and others, to give their lives rather than pledge allegiance to a false god.

Gathering on Sunday Proclaims the Sovereignty and Presence of the Risen Christ

Sunday is the Lord's day, the day of Christ's resurrection. This "little Easter" is a day of freedom and liberation from death. It is a day to renew and reaffirm our commitment to Christ, who stands as our liberator from sin, death, and everything that enslaves and shackles people.

Sunday was the day the early church experienced the presence of Christ in a special way. They gathered to tell stories of Christ, to pray and to break bread together. In the same way the church today gathers to celebrate and affirm Christ present among the people of God: *Where two or three are gath-*

ered in my name, there I am in the midst of them (Matthew 18:19–20).

Earlier generations also named Sunday "the eighth day," the first day of new creation following the resurrection. The renewal, healing and recommitment which hopefully attend our communal worship are the continuation of God's act of creation and of Christ's act of re-creation. As disciples we are called to carry to the whole world the healing we experience through our worship.

In all of these Sunday elements the reign or kingdom of God is present. Like a diamond flashing light, each facet represents a different aspect. Look at Sunday one way and one discerns the reign of God shattering the power of death and freeing God's covenant people from the tyrany of death. View Sunday another way and one observes the Christian community celebrating *as if* God's reign had begun, *as if* Christ were *already* King of Creation, Lord of the Nations, *as if* all the community were equal and welcome at God's throne. Hold it yet another way and one recognizes our common need to rest, to be re-created and recentered in our lives, to remind ourselves that we are creatures and to offer to our Creator our prayer, praise and thanksgiving.

Our Sunday Gathering Affirms the Values of the Sabbath

Genesis declares that God blessed the sabbath, making time sacred (Genesis 2:3). The Christian community inherited many gifts from the Jewish observance of shabat or sabbath. Among these gifts are: rest from work, time for renewal and recreation, worship, being with family and friends, care and concern for others, and hospitable welcome to all. There are justice implications here. Consider only the need to cease from work, to rest, to give replenishment to the workers. Indeed, humanity is placed in its proper context of the whole creation when one recalls that Deuteronomy extends sabbath justice themes to extend rest and release to creation and to the land, as well as to slaves and debts (Deuteronomy 15).

Our Mission and Ministry

In Our Gathering We Show Care for One Another

When we acknowledge the presence of others who also gather for Sunday worship, when we smile and say "Good morning," when we sit with others instead of by ourselves, when we help others with coats, books or bulletins, we are expressing mutual care for one another. This care and concern is one way of recognizing and honoring the presence of Christ in another person. Such gracious and hospitable practice is one means of embodying the teachings of Jesus in Matthew

At the end of every seven years you shall grant a release. And this is the manner of the release: every creditor shall release what he has lent to his neighbour; he shall not exact it of his neighbour, his brother, because the Lord's release has been proclaimed. Of a foreigner you may exact it; but whatever of yours is with your brother your hand shall release. But there will be no poor among you (for the LORD will bless you in the land which the LORD your God gives you for an inheritance to possess), if only you will obey the voice of the LORD your God, being careful to do all this commandment which I command you this day.

Deuteronomy 15:1–5

Thus heaven and earth were completed with all their array. On the seventh day God completed the work he had been doing. He rested on the seventh day after all the work he had been doing. God blessed the seventh day and made it holy, because on that day he had rested after all his work of creating.

Genesis 2:1–3

42

Through his cross and resurrection
he freed us from sin and death
and called us to the glory that has made us
a chosen race, a royal priesthood,
a holy nation, a people set apart.[7]

Loving God, we offer you
this bread and this cup,
remembering his death
and celebrating his resurrection.
You have made him the light of the nations,
and the bearer of justice to the ends of the
     earth.
Therefore we proclaim our hope.[8]

25, to show care and concern for the least of Jesus' brothers and sisters as a routine part of our ministries and lives.

In Our Gathering the Many Different Gifts Are Brought Together Into Unity

Though there is a radical equality within the assembly of the baptized, there are also many different gifts. The Spirit richly endows the community with gifts for the many different ministries that are required for a full Christian life. These gifts include preaching, teaching, presiding, hospitable presence, singing, playing musical instruments, serving, welcoming and praying, among others.

Some of these gifts are exercised mainly in the life of the Christian community during the week. Some, however, are also exercised especially during the Sunday liturgy.

In Our Gathering We Acknowledge that We Are Sinners

To acknowledge our weakness and failures is, of course, to say something of who we are as God's people. However, such an acknowledgment also has to do with our mission and ministry. We confess that we are a part of the problem in our world. We admit that there are things we have done that have contributed to society's problems and that there are some things we have left undone which could have addressed those problems. In our confession we remind ourselves that we cannot be superior to those for whom we might feel condemnation. In our confession we bring to our remembrance our need to depend upon God's action and strength to sustain our ministries and our faith.

But we make our confession and acknowledge our sinfulness within the context of a baptismal relationship with God. We make our confession confident not only that God will hear and receive, but that God will also forgive and heal us.

Reflect On This Vision

Our vision of the relationship between the liturgy of gathering and social justice may be summarized as follows:

> The People Who Worship
>   We gather because we are called
>   Our gathering emphasizes community
>   Our gathering is an experience of radical
>   equality
>   In our gathering children are hospitably
>   welcomed
>   Our gathering is characterized by joy and hope

The God We Worship
    Our gathering names God as true God
    Gathering on Sunday proclaims the sovereignty
       and presence of the risen Christ
    Our Sunday gathering affirms the values of the
       sabbath

Our Mission and Ministry
    In our gathering we show care for one another.
    In our gathering the many different gifts are
       brought together into unity
    In our gathering we acknowledge that we are
       sinners

In what respects does this vision agree with and affirm your own understanding of the connection between Sunday worship and social justice?

What ideas regarding this relationship are new to you? How do you react to them?

The Liturgical Celebration

The vision of the church's best experience and greatest wisdom regarding the gathering liturgy as a whole, and its relationship to social justice, is in practice expressed, worked out and implemented in the various specific elements that comprise the liturgy of gathering. We therefore need to consider these individual elements one by one.

In addition, we recognize that the vision of the relationship between social justice and the gathering liturgy seldom if ever entirely coincides with our actual experience on Sunday morning. The question then becomes: How can we change our actual practice so that vision and experience are in greater accord? To evaluate and improve our Sunday liturgy we likewise need to examine the individual elements that go to make up the liturgy of gathering as a whole.

Genuine hospitality is a very rich concept. . . . Hospitality has to penetrate and humanize the entire building: the harmony of its materials, the scale of its proportions, the totality of its internal and external relations. Nothing truly human is indifferent to hospitality.

Frederic Debuyst[9]

Rune of Hospitality

I saw a stranger yestreen:
I put food in the eating place,
drink in the drinking place,
music in the listening place;
and in the blessed name of the Triune
he blessed myself and my house,
my cattle and my dear ones,
and the lark said in her song
    often, often, often,
goes the Christ in the stranger's guise
    often, often, often,
goes the Christ in the stranger's guise.

An Old Gaelic Rune[10]

If a poor man or a poor woman comes, whether they are from your own parish or from another, above all if they are advanced in years, and if there is no room for them, make a place for them, O bishop, with all your heart, even if you yourself have to sit on the ground.

    You must not make any distinction between persons if you wish your ministry to be pleasing before God.

Didascalia of the Apostles[11]

NON-VERBAL DIMENSIONS

The first area of possible improvement to examine is that of the environment of worship: its non-verbal dimensions. This environment has two aspects, that of human relationships—we will call this "hospitality"—and that of the architecture of the church building.

Hospitality

How are battered women cared for in your community?

What is being done to welcome refugees and immigrants and help them find homes and jobs?

What do you think should be done to help teenagers who run away from home?

Hospitality, like all of worship, involves people. Hospitality basically means welcoming, paying attention to, honoring and valuing one another. We are invited to practice hospitality because God was and is first hospitable to us, welcoming us in baptism into God's family.

If an aim of the gathering liturgy is to promote and bring about unity, to make us ready for word and sacrament, then it is absolutely essential that we be attentive to one another, acknowledge one another's presence, be glad that others are present together, and be eager to join with others in the common worship.

As a community, we need to be hospitable to women and men; to infants, children and teens; to those with physical or mental disabilities; to strangers, guests, those who are only tentatively present; to all regardless of position, economic status or the lack thereof. Furthermore, in the 18th chapter of Matthew's gospel, Jesus reminds us that the "little ones" of the community, that is, those who are dependent in any way, are to be brought into the center of the community, and that the community is one of people who forgive one another.

Hospitality is a form of social justice, for it is the practice of radical equality of human beings before God and of caring for all God's people. The divisions within society must be overcome, even destroyed, as all are welcomed into God's covenant community. Such hospitality is a way of "playing" or rehearsing the reign of God in such a way that such values might form and characterize our lives and ministries on Monday and Tuesday as well.

The primary obligation for practicing hospitality clearly applies to every member of the community. As people gather, it is appropriate to speak to others, smile across the room, give a friendly nod. Such hospitality is not irreverent, for you are being reverent to people, honoring the Christ that is present in them. Many will welcome the opportunity to sit with others instead of finding a place in a corner by themselves. They should be pleased to sit in the center of a row of seats, thus inviting others to join them, instead of on the aisle in a more unwelcoming manner.

The community can also see to its needs for hospitality by designating certain of its members to minister on its behalf. Such greeters, or ministers of hospitality, are very important. Thus a family, or groups of individuals, including children, the elderly and the disabled, may be involved in greeting people upon their arrival, assisting with coats, introducing visitors, guiding strangers with worship books or aids, showing persons to their seats; all are elements of hospitable ministry.

Architecture

What is being done in your city to make grocery stores, sports facilities, public restrooms, etc. accessible to people in wheelchairs?

How are blind or deaf people being helped to find satisfactory employment?

The second component of the environment of worship is the physical space of the church and its architectural design. This is significant as one of the ways in which the community exercises hospitality, and it is also an important means of expressing the self-identity of the community as local church.

Architecture, or the physical arrangement of the worship space, can either help or hinder the practice of hospitable gathering. Consider the access to the church itself. A small, suburban church was once featured on a poster. It was a typical church: white frame, steeple, double doors. Leading up to it was a twin flight of steps, maybe two dozen stairs. At the bottom of the steps sat a young girl in a wheelchair looking up at the church. Does our worship space invite people in and make it accessible for them, or does it mock and impede them?

Churches need gathering spaces (called, for example, the narthex or foyer) in addition to that space set aside for worship. An increasing number of architects are suggesting that a church's narthex should be at least as large as the worship space. It is there that the community interacts, engages one another before and after worship, where mutual conversation and consolation occur, where the stranger is welcomed, the newly baptized embraced.

Such a gathering place, among other features, needs a place for coats. Without ample room for hanging their coats,

Auto Body Shop

The building we now occupy was chosen mainly for its size and location in our neighborhood. It is a single story brick structure, originally a car dealership and later an auto body shop. Our fellowship crew did most of the remodeling.

The meetinghouse contains a large area for worship. On one side is a half circle of elevated risers on which we place chairs for about 350 people. During services and other functions the worship leader and our music group complete the circle. A space behind the music group provides more congregational seating. We've found the circular seating arrangement highly effective because it both enhances the spirit of unity as well as greatly improves visibility.

In the open area in the center of the circle we have ample space for creative movement, interpretive dance, and drama. These three are now meaningful aspects of our worship. Underneath this center area, covered by a carpeted lid, is our baptism pool, a circular concrete structure with stairs curving down one side.

Our meetinghouse is also used for Friday evening community meals when adults and their guests share dinner together. The extensive floor space and our roomy kitchen allow well over 100 people to dine together comfortably. One room is used as a food co-op while another provides space for a play group for two and three year olds.

Bob Crepeau[12]

Two excellent resources on architecture and liturgy:

Environment and Art in Catholic Worship (Washington: United States Catholic Conferences 1978)

Visual Art in the Life of the Church: Encouraging Creative Worship and Witness in the Congregation, by Richard Caemmerer (Augsburg Publishing House 1983)

Some Liturgical Spaces Suitable for Eucharistic Celebration[13]

1.

A U-shaped seating arrangement around a central table and gathering space. Pulpit/lectern and font are located on either side of table. This may be a new building or an alteration of an old central pulpit/organ/choir space.

2.

Communion table in corner. Platform and furniture may be portable so as to allow a variety of arrangements.

3.

Altered use of cruciform shape with table and pulpit moved out of the chancel into the crossing. The nave may be shortened and the chancel closed off to form a small meeting room or overflow space (if moveable partitions are used). Increasing the size of the narthex by shortening the length of the nave creates a very valuable meeting space for people before and after the service.

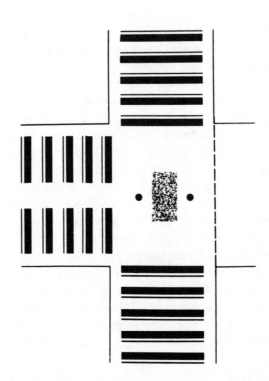

4.

Altered use of longitudinal nave with table placed along one side wall and chairs or pews arranged to form a hollow U.

people are encouraged to leave them on. To thus wear one's coat images a tentative participation in worship, for it non-verbally communicates the intention to leave speedily, or that one is only reluctantly present, or that one does not want to be touched or involved. Do you leave your coat on when you visit in a friend's home?

Within the worship space itself, architecture can facilitate or obstruct the gathering of individuals into a unified community. Row upon row of statically arranged pews in which one studies the back of the head in front isolates individuals and is destructive of community. In constrast, a dynamic, interactive seating plan allows eye contact, encourages awareness of other people gathered around the same word and sacrament, and promotes a sense of community.

In addition, architecture must not create barriers or areas of status that are incompatible with the radical equality of the baptized community. For example, if the presiding minister's seat is considerably higher than the rest of the community, is it communicating ease of visibility and more effective leadership, or a higher status? Some congregations have fence-like communion rails separating altar from people, or completely surrounding the table; the image given is more "barrier" than "holy space."

Finally, the participation of the assembly in worship is very much influenced by such factors as visibility, audibility, and ease of movement. Can everyone see the place(s) of proclamation and preaching, the baptismal font, the altar or table, the minister? Can everyone hear what is spoken or sung? Are aisles and seating spaced so that people can move as required?

What's Happening Now?

Think about the ways you personally experience hospitality at your Sunday worship. Do you practice hospitality?

To what extent do you experience and value the "informal" phase of the liturgy of gathering as part of an important community-building process? Do you intend to worship as a member of the local church community or simply as a private individual?

In what ways do you experience hope and joy during Sunday worship?

To what extent are you conscious of the architectural setting of your Sunday liturgy and how it influences your worship? What message regarding human relationships and community is given by the architecture of your church?

Do you experience "radical equality" and "community" while at worship? After you have answered this question for yourself, then answer it in these ways:

> *If you are a man, answer as a woman;*
> *an adult, as a teenager;*
> *older, as a child;*
> *employed, as an unemployed person;*
> *healthy, as a person experiencing illness or*
>   *disability;*
> *well-known, as someone who experiences isolation.*

Are The Connections Being Made?

How well do the non-verbal dimensions of the gathering liturgy express social justice values? Fail to express them? Contradict them?

Are There Changes To Be Made?

Identify practices of gathering that are good and that you want to affirm, support and see continued. How will you support these?

Identify practices that need to be improved, corrected or changed. What alternatives to these practices can you envision? What can you do to bring about these changes?

If You Have Energy For Just One Area, Start Here

If there is no welcoming or hospitality committee, start one.
or
Seek out a person or cluster of persons who tend to be "invisible" within your church community. Spend some time getting to know of their experiences. Invite their input and fuller participation in the workings of your church community.

VERBAL DIMENSIONS

The more formal, verbal part of the gathering liturgy also needs to be examined carefully, in order to see how its individual elements communicate our vision of the relationship of liturgy to social justice, and to consider how they might need to be improved.

Song

Singing is an important part of this phase of the gathering liturgy. Quite apart from what actually is sung, an opening song serves an important purpose as another unifying, community-building element, as all raise their voices together to praise God musically at the beginning of Sunday worship. Its melody, rhythm and pace, as well as words, also help to set the mood of the liturgy.

Song. We use the term *song* for any piece of vocal music used in the liturgy. Though the term *hymn* in a narrow sense really refers to a particular type of musical composition, we follow popular usage in sometimes using it simply as a synonym for *song*.

The Authors

50

Music and Liturgy

Among the many signs and symbols used by the Church to celebrate its faith, music is of preeminent importance . . . music should assist the assembled believers to express and share the gift of faith that is within them and to nourish and strengthen their interior commitment of faith.

It should heighten the texts so that they speak more fully and more effectively. The quality and joy and enthusiasm which music adds to community worship cannot be gained in any other way. It imparts a sense of unity to the congregation and sets the appropriate tone for a particular celebration.

Music, in addition to expressing texts, can also unveil a dimension of meaning and feeling, a communication of ideas and intuitions which words alone cannot yield. This dimension is integral to the human personality and to [our] growth in faith. It cannot be ignored if the signs of worship are to speak to the whole person.

Music in Catholic Worship[14]

Music and Social Justice

Common problems with traditional music for worship, from a social justice point of view, include: non-inclusive language, inappropriate images of God, military images, excessive individualism, and an other-worldly orientation.

Relatively little music that is oriented to social justice is in common use in the churches; what there is needs to be promoted and made more widely known.

Music oriented to social justice should not be manipulative, necessarily will have a prophetic perspective, and can include protest songs or eschatological songs, prophetically envisioning a new world reality and announcing it here and now.

As with any music used in worship, that oriented to social justice must also respect the nature of the liturgy and the liturgical occasion on which it is used. In addition, it should be good music, and within the capabilities of the musicians and congregation using it.

The Authors

There is a growing library of music relating justice and liturgy, including:

What Will We Do? Songs of Hunger and Justice. (Philadelphia: Lutheran Church in America Division for Parish Services, 1983.)

Renew Us, Lord: Songs of Christian Commitment. (Schiller Park, Illinois: World Library Publications, Inc., 1985.) Includes songs related to world peace, justice, ecology, disarmament and personal peace.

Freedom Is Coming: Songs of Protest and Praise from South Africa. Collected and edited by Anders Nyberg. (Chapel Hill: Hinshaw Music, 1985.)

The text of the opening song may relate to the scripture readings, season or feast, the fact that there will be baptism that day, or help prepare for the preaching, or reflect particular concerns that will be raised up in worship. The text of this song may of course include social justice themes explicitly, and its language should be inclusive and contain a rich range of images of God.

It is also important to recognize the social justice implications of songs that are traditionally used in the gathering liturgy, such as the ancient Christian hymn, "Glory to God in the highest." Though this usually goes unnoticed because it is so familiar, many social justice themes are implicit in its text: the song of the angels sung to the poor, socially marginalized shepherds who worked in a land occupied by a foreign power; the declaration of peace for God's people on earth; the proclamation of God as the Sovereign One; and the imagery of Christ as the paschal lamb, which brings to our remembrance God's liberation of the people of God from slavery and death.

Greeting

To what extent do you think that people in your city give their allegiance to money, sports, power, pleasure, television?

Some communities begin the formal gathering with a scripture sentence, others with an apostolic greeting, or the sign of the cross, or various combinations of these. The point is to declare right at the beginning that this gathering of God's people is in God's name, at God's gracious invitation.

It is then appropriate for the presider to welcome the people more informally and more personally, and perhaps to speak briefly to the focus or particular orientation of that day's liturgy. It is appropriate also to acknowledge the presence of the children during these remarks. This personal and less formal greeting invites all present to participate fully in the Sunday worship.

Confession or Reminder of Baptism

How are persons released from prison helped to find jobs and homes?

Another common element of the gathering liturgy is corporate confession followed by absolution or assurance of forgiveness, of which the litany, "Lord, have mercy," may be a part. Sometimes it is important and useful to acknowledge and confess that we have failed to recognize who we are as the people of God, who our God is whom we worship, and to what ministry we have been called. Thus the confession can deal explicitly with the vision of liturgy and social justice enunciated above, and can be phrased not only in individual and personal terms, but also in communal and socially conscious ways.

Sometimes it is valid and useful to construct the penitential rite or confession so that it expresses praise for God's mercy and for the forgiveness which is shown to us daily. After all, we are also a redeemed people, and confession needs to be balanced by joy, by a reminder of our call to be God's own people and God's hands in the world of today. In some churches the presider may lead the confession prior to the entrance hymn, or may do so while stationed at the baptismal font or at the entrance. Another alternative is to place the confession so that it is a response to the proclamation and preaching of the word of God.

Some churches provide an alternative to the confession in the form of an explicit reminder of one's baptismal identity. A prayer may be prayed which brings to one's remembrance God's many acts of redemption that are associated with water, especially with one's own baptism; the people are then sprinkled with this water in remembrance of their baptism.

Prayer

To what extent are ordinary individuals listened to when important decisions are made by your town council?

In the name of the Father, and of the Son, and of the Holy Spirit.

The grace of our Lord Jesus Christ, the love of God, and the communion of the Holy Spirit be with you all.[15]

Alleluia. Christ is risen. The Lord is risen indeed. Alleluia.[16]

May his grace and peace be with you, May he fill our hearts with joy.[17]

Most merciful God, we confess that we are in bondage to sin and cannot free ourselves. We have sinned against you in thought, word, and deed, by what we have done and by what we have left undone. We have not loved you with our whole heart; we have not loved our neighbors as ourselves. For the sake of your Son, Jesus Christ, have mercy on us. Forgive us, renew us, and lead us, so that we may delight in your will and walk in your ways, to the glory of your holy name. Amen.[18]

Blessing and Sprinkling Holy Water

Dear friends,
this water will be used
to remind us of our baptism.
Let us ask God to bless it,
and to keep us faithful
to the Spirit he has given us.

. . . your gift of water
brings life and freshness to the earth;
it washes away our sins
and brings us eternal life.

We ask you now
to bless this water,
and to give us your protection on this day
which you have made your own.
Renew the living spring of your life within us
and protect us in spirit and body,
that we may be free from sin
and come into your presence
to receive your gift of salvation.

We ask this through Christ our Lord. Amen.

May almighty God cleanse us of our sins,
and through the eucharist we celebrate
make us worthy to sit at his table
in his heavenly kingdom. Amen.[19]

The transition from the gathering liturgy to the liturgy of the word is marked by prayer. Called the "collect," or "prayer of the day," or "opening prayer," this brief prayer collects the prayers of the people as they begin their worship, and may refer to the season or feast.

In some churches this prayer is said aloud by all the people, or responsively by minister and congregation. In others the congregation prays silently, after which the minister enunciates a spoken prayer.

In the latter case, the presider may, with gesture and speech, declare, "The Lord be with you," to which the assembly in dialogue replies, "And also with you." The presider then gives the invitation, "Let us pray." The community then proceeds to pray in silence, as they are so moved; it is important to allow ample time for this, otherwise the people are deprived of their proper participation in this prayer.

Most often, these prayers are rather general in content. Some, however, are more explicit, and laden with social justice imagery. For example, this prayer of the day for December 28, commemorating the Holy Innocents:

We remember today, O God, the slaughter of the holy innocents of Bethlehem by order of King Herod. Receive, we pray, into the arms of your mercy all innocent victims, and by your great might frustrate the designs of evil tyrants and establish your rule of justice, love and peace; through Jesus Christ our Lord, who lives and reigns with you and the Holy Spirit, one God, now and forever. Amen.[20]

Or this prayer of the day for the Fourth Sunday of Easter:

God of all power, you called from death our Lord Jesus, the great shepherd of the sheep. Send us as shepherds to rescue the lost, to heal the injured, and to feed one another with knowledge and understanding; through your Son, Jesus Christ our Lord, who lives and reigns with you and with the Holy Spirit, one God, now and forever.[21]

The gathered people of God are now ready to celebrate the liturgy of the word.

What's Happening Now?

At next Sunday's liturgy, notice if the singing during the gathering liturgy brings people together and builds community. De-

scribe the images of God and people contained in the songs and hymns. What do you think about these?

To what extent do you find the "confession" that is included in the Sunday liturgy meaningful, and speaking to your own situation? To what extent is it liberating, reminding you that you are forgiven?

In what ways are you ever reminded of your baptism at the beginning of Sunday worship, and do you value this? How?

Is sufficient time allowed for you to participate in the opening prayer, both silently and aloud?

If you sit in the pew, describe the type of relationship that exists between your presider and congregation during worship. If you are the presider, describe the relationship as you see and communicate it during worship.

Are The Connections Being Made?

How well do the verbal and structural elements of the gathering liturgy of your own Sunday liturgy express social justice values? Fail to express them? Contradict them?

Are There Changes To Be Made?

Identify aspects of the verbal, structured part of the liturgy of gathering that are good and that you want to affirm, support and see continued. How will you support these?

Identify practices that need to be improved, corrected or changed. What alternatives to these practices can you envision? What can you do to bring about these changes?

If You Have Energy For Just One Area, Start Here:

Work toward the use of songs that use inclusive language and a broad range of images of God.
or
Begin occasionally to start worship with a reminder of baptism instead of confession.

5. The Liturgy of the Word

Introduction

The Liturgy of the Word and Social Justice

   The God We Worship
      In the liturgy of the word, the worshiping people first of all encounter Christ
      In the word proclaimed and preached, we are reminded who our God really is
      The word proclaims the reign of God

   The People Who Worship
      The word of God proclaimed and preached is therefore for disciples, the baptized
      The word of God is received as gift
      The word of God both denounces and announces

   Our Mission and Ministry
      The word of God inspires us with the example of Jesus' own ministry
      The word shows us how Jesus prepared his disciples to minister in his name

The Liturgical Celebration

   Non-Verbal Dimensions
      Architecture
      Sharing of ministry

   Verbal Dimensions
      Proclaiming the word
      Preaching the word
      Responding to the word
         The psalm
         Sharing and witnessing
         The creed
         Prayers of intercession
         Offering or collection
         Sign of peace and confession

56

Sermon. Churches favor different terms to name the preaching of the word. Without making any judgment upon these diverse usages, we will use *sermon* and *homily* interchangeably.

Proclamation. We have used *proclamation* in the narrow sense of the public reading of scripture within the liturgy; this allows us readily to distinguish between such reading of the biblical word, and preaching based on it. In a broader sense of the word, *proclamation* also includes preaching and indeed other aspects of the liturgy.

The Authors

The people of God, the church, come together, become visible and express their self-identity in the gathering liturgy. Once gathered, they proceed to the second phase of Sunday worship, the liturgy of the word.

The basic structure of the liturgy of the word is quite simple: the proclamation and preaching of the word, followed by the responses of the gathered people to that word. In practice these elements are interspersed. A psalm or hymn may be a response to the first scripture reading. A short period of silence is a frequent response to the second scripture reading. In at least some churches, a sung acclamation whose principal theme is "Alleluia" prepares the assembly for the third reading. This third scripture reading is the climax of the three texts and is from the gospels. The preaching of the word follows. In some churches, a hymn is sung as an immediate response to the sermon or homily.

Three final responses to the word follow. The first is the profession of faith or creed, in which we again state our allegiance to the one true God. The second consists of prayers: intercessions for the church, the world and those in any need. The third is the offering, or collection, in which we contribute financially or materially to help the poor, those in need, the many for whom we have just prayed.

Though the liturgy of the word by its very nature is highly verbal, there are also several important non-verbal components. One of these is music, which is often the medium of the congregation's response to the word. A second consists of the architectural, artistic and physical setting for the liturgy of the word. Finally, the word is proclaimed and responded to by the way ministry is shared and the manner in which the assembly participates.

What Is Your Own Experience

Think about your own experience of the liturgy of the word. What meaning does it have for you?

Describe what actually happens as you and your community celebrate the liturgy of the word.

The Liturgy of the Word and Social Justice

What vision of the liturgy of the word does the wisdom of the Christian tradition set before us? What ought we to study and ponder regarding the word and its liturgical proclamation and celebration? What does this vision tell us regarding the deep and intrinsic relationship that exists between the word and social justice?

The God We Worship

In the Liturgy of the Word, the Worshiping People First of all Encounter Christ

Christ is mediated through proclamation and preaching. They then respond to this encounter. The community's encounter with, and response to the word of God is forceful and transforming.

In the liturgy of the word the worshiping assembly listens and responds to the word of God proclaimed and preached. By announcing that "the Word became flesh and dwelt with us, full of grace and truth," the gospel of John (1:14) reminds us that the word of God is first of all the person of Jesus Christ. In the liturgy of the word, Christ is present in scripture and preaching, as well as in the response of his body, the church.

The word of God, then, clearly is powerful, but its power is of life, not domination. Encountering the word of God becomes an experience of conversion for the gathered assembly, an experience of the call to turn one's life and the life of the community more completely toward God.

The scriptural word bears the story of God's relationship with creation and with God's people in the past. The preached word carries that story into the present. The sermon or homily thus joins ancient stories of God's people to contemporary stories of God's people who seek to be faithful in this age. All this leads to confidence that God's loving and faithful relationship with God's people and with all of creation will continue into the future.

In the Word Proclaimed and Preached, We Are Reminded Who Our God Really Is

The one living God—not any political, social or economic ideology, not a human ruler or system—was manifested in Jesus Christ, the child of God. The word of God confronts, challenges and shatters the temptations we may have to serve idols of nation, person or social standing.

We give you thanks, O God, through your beloved Servant, Jesus Christ. It is he who you have sent in these last times to save us and redeem us, and be the messenger of your will. He is your Word, inseparable from you, through whom you made all things and in whom you take delight.[1]

God of power and might, we praise you through your Son, Jesus Christ, who comes in your name. He is the Word that brings salvation. He is the hand you stretch out to sinners. He is the way that leads to your peace.[2]

We give you thanks and praise, almighty God, through your beloved Son, Jesus Christ, our Saviour and Redeemer. He is your living Word, through whom you have created all things.[3]

58

The Mustard Seed and the Yeast

(Matthew 13:31–35)

MANUEL: "It seems to me that the word of God is a very delicate thing, very tiny. At first it seems insignificant and therefore many people despise it, but afterwards it grows like a mustard tree. And so at first Jesus spoke his word to twelve people, and that was very insignificant, but it spread to others and was as scattered throughout the world. And it has spread so far it has reached even us in Solentiname. It also seems to me that the word of God is tiny and insignificant because it sprouts in our hearts and you almost can't see it. But then I tell it to someone else, and so it grows and spreads like a great tree, and this tree is the transformation of the world."

The Gospel in Solentiname[4]

For the gifts of mercy and new life:
Through the waters of the Red Sea
you delivered us from suffering and servitude;
at the foot of your sacred mountain
you called us to truth and holiness;
in the words of your holy prophets
you called us to justice and compassion;
through the lives of your blessed saints and
* martyrs*
you taught us wisdom and faithfulness.[5]

In the fullness of time you sent your Son,
born of a woman to be our Saviour.
He was wounded for our transgressions,
and bruised for our iniquities.
He opened to us the way of freedom and
* peace.*[6]

The Word Proclaims the Reign of God

We, the church are called to prepare for God's reign. While we cannot make it come or achieve it of our own efforts, the proclaimed word invites us to experience and practice "kingdom values" already as we journey in faith. The image of the reign of God set before us is of relationships transformed between God and humankind, among individuals and nations, and between humanity and creation. While this reign of God in its fullness and wholeness is of the future, in our worship we are called and invited to a foretaste of it in the present. The gathered community experiences that foretaste in its worship life through word and sacrament.

In the world one encounters hostility among people and nations, suspicion of the stranger, unjust divisions of goods and wealth, oppression of the poor and categories of people, the reign of death. In the liturgy, one encounters peace shared, hospitable welcome to the stranger, equitable sharing of bread and wine, equality among baptized people, the celebration of life in spite of death. Such kingdom attributes are borne into the midst of the assembly by the story of God and proclaimed in preaching. Such values challenge us as people and as the church. The liturgical modeling of the kingdom will shape our ministry, it will form and inform our witness and daily living in the world.

The People Who Worship

The Word of God Proclaimed and Preached Is Therefore for Disciples, the Baptized

This word embraces, sustains and encourages those who have followed Jesus, who have been sent out by Jesus in ministry during the week. This word renews our vision, heals our wounds and comforts us, forgives our weakness and failures, challenges us to conversion, encourages our ministry, empowers us for mission, and sustains our life. It is part of the continuing ministry of Christ to his disciples, to those who will follow Jesus, who will be sent out by him in ministry in the week to come.

The Word of God Is Received as Gift

This gift is neither restricted nor manipulated. The word's action in communities and individuals is as mysterious as the biblical grain of wheat sown, as the growth of the mustard seed. This gift, though, is like a two-edged sword: it both denounces and announces.

The Word of God Both Denounces and Announces

The word of God, proclaimed and preached, is unambiguous about injustice, oppression, the exploitation of the created order, including humankind. It rails against those who pretend to serve God and wealth. It confronts the church, the people of God, with the call to faithfulness, the mandate to live lives in conformity with God's reign. The word of God denounces the world's bad news and condemns the covenant community when God's covenant is forgotten or broken.

But the word also announces the gospel, the good news. It is equally unambiguous about the prodigal nature of God's grace, God's longing to love, forgive and uphold the people of God, the almost fairy tale-like news of life beyond death, of eternal relationship with God through Christ.

Our Mission and Ministry

The Word of God Inspires Us with the Example of Jesus' Own Ministry

We are called through baptism to continue the ministry of Jesus, to be his hands and voice in today's world. How else can we do this unless we learn from scripture the many stories in which Jesus gives his personal example of ministry? Through the word read and preached we encounter Jesus and examples of his ministry. The story of Jesus feeding the multitudes images the shape of our ministry in a hungry world. The story of Jesus teaching the crowds gives structure and content to the church's ministry of teaching. The stories of Jesus at prayer offer insight to our own life of prayer.

The Word Shows Us How Jesus Prepared His Disciples to Minister in His Name

The gospel narratives teach us how to become ministering disciples. They give us many stories of how Jesus trained his friends to carry on his ministry after his death. The examples of servanthood, faith and discipleship which Jesus presented to his disciples become the means by which we are upheld as disciples of Jesus. The story of Peter's denial and subsequent ministry comforts and sustains us in our times of temptation and uncertainty. The gospels bear the story of Jesus' commands into our own contemporary contexts: "Do this in memory of me"; "Go therefore into all the world baptizing and teaching."

Reflect On This Vision

Our vision of the relationship between the liturgy of the word and social justice may be summarized as follows:

The God We Worship

In the preaching of the church and in the celebration of the sacraments the tendency toward individual self-interest and toward excluding large parts of human experience from what we call "the life of grace" must be constantly overcome. There is no such thing as "spiritual life" or "life in Christ" apart from all the relationships that make up human life in the communities in which we live and serve.

John Egan[7]

To envisage the liturgy as rehearsing and celebrating a story of God independent of the stories of the people who participate is simply to perpetuate the split between faith and life, between the actions of the liturgy and the manifold activities that make up our lives as human beings. How can you revise the story of the liturgy to make it inclusive of the hopes and fears, sufferings and aspirations of today's world?

John Egan[8]

When . . . we have some capacity for feeling the suffering, the hunger, the want of not just an abstract humanity but our sisters and brothers around the globe—their terror under the constant threat of annihilation, their oppression by the military-industrial complex on the one hand and by other totalitarian systems on the other—then we can begin to see the social consequences of the Mass.

Robert W. Hovda[9]

In the liturgy of the word, the worshiping people
  first of all encounter Christ
In the word proclaimed and preached, we are
  reminded who our God is
The word proclaims the reign of God
The People Who Worship
  The word of God proclaimed and preached is
    therefore for disciples, the baptized
  The word of God is received as gift
  The word of God both denounces and announces
Our Mission and Ministry
  The word of God inspires us with the example of
    Jesus' own ministry
  The word shows us how Jesus prepared his
    disciples to minister in his name

In what respects does this vision agree with and affirm your own understanding of the connection between Sunday worship and social justice?

What ideas regarding this relationship are new to you? How do you react to them?

The Liturgical Celebration

The vision of the church's best experience and wisdom regarding the liturgy of the word probably does not entirely coincide with our actual experience on Sunday morning.

We therefore need to ask: How can we change our actual practice so that vision and experience are in greater accord? How can we improve our Sunday liturgy? How can we make the community's encounter with the word of God as forceful and as transforming as possible (remembering of course that ultimately God is at work here, and that it is God's gift, grace and action that are important)?

NON-VERBAL DIMENSIONS

The first area of possible improvement to examine is that of the non-verbal dimensions of the liturgy of the word, especially the question of architecture and that of the sharing of ministries.

Architecture

What is being done to provide adequate housing for persons who are economically poor?

Do caretakers and janitors receive adequate wages in your community? health insurance? pensions?

How are artists encouraged and supported in your area?

The architectural setting for the liturgy of the word carries both an interpretation of what the word is, and also an interpretation of who we are who listen and respond.

The arrangement of the space in which the word is proclaimed and preached influences the meaning it has for the assembly. For example, some churches are arranged like courtrooms, others like lecture halls, and still others like theaters. In such cases, the emphasis seems to be on the word coming as judgment, as teaching, or as a call to initial conversion to Christ. All three models place the word and its minister in opposition, over against the people. In such arrangements, the people have a rather passive role as spectators; their active participation is discouraged, for communication is essentially a one-way monologue.

Better arrangements might be suggested by the examples of the campfire, the family living room, or a circle beneath a tree, settings in which the family or community gathers around the elder sister or brother telling the story. The community is dynamically engaged, their participation and response is encouraged and facilitated, for communication is through dialogue.

The arrangement of our worship space, including congregational seating, also says something about who we think Jesus is, for it is Jesus' voice we hear, his message that is preached. Is he judge, teacher, evangelist, master, friend? Is he distant and strange, or a close and intimate figure? In part, all are correct; but where is the emphasis?

The arrangement also says something about how we see ourselves. Are we sinners to be judged, unbelievers needing conversion to Christ, redeemed sinners, believers, disciples, the baptized people of God called to be ministers of Christ?

Preparation

Though the Word often surprises us, the Liturgy of the Word benefits from preparation. The use of a lectionary, an ordered guide to scripture readings patterned into the seasons of the Church Year, immersed in the Paschal Mystery, can aid that preparation. For with a lectionary, all are aware of the readings assigned for the coming Sunday or Festival.

Preparation may take the form of a bible study, the reading of the texts as part of one's personal or family devotions, the reading of scripture with others of the community followed by reflection and discussion or encouraging our personal prayer to arise from the Word. The community should be informed of the readings to be proclaimed next Sunday and be encouraged to read them ahead of time. In addition, we need to learn and practice the arts of storytelling and of story-listening in families, communities, and in our daily lives.

Preparatory reading of the texts is especially important for the involvement of children in worship. Through their familiarity with the stories, children are better equipped to share in worship for they will pick up familiar names, words or plots as the texts are proclaimed. It is but one way of honoring the presence of children in worship. Older children may use that preparation to be included among the readers on a given Sunday.

The Authors

Pulpit. In different churches the word may be proclaimed and preached from one, two or even three distinct places within the church building. The principle piece of furniture used—a raised reading stand—is usually called *pulpit* or *ambo*. A secondary reading stand often is called a *lectern*.

Reader. The person or persons who proclaim the scripture word are variously called the *reader* or *lector*.

The Authors

Again, all of these are, in part, correct. But where is the emphasis? Is that the emphasis we intend? Might we even wish to change the worship and seating arrangement to provide different emphases during the various seasons of the church year?

The place from which the word is proclaimed and preached is part of this architectural consideration, for it has a significant symbolic and functional role. An imposing pulpit, or ambo, speaks non-verbally of the power and importance the word has for us. But it can also serve to distance the word from the people, diminish their active participation, or hierarchically elevate the preacher. The practice in some churches of processing into the midst of the congregation for the gospel reading dramatically and symbolically places Jesus among his people, and gives a certain priority to the assembly as a presence of Christ.

Similarly, the book from which the word is read bears important non-verbal meaning. A large, handsomely bound Bible or lectionary, perhaps honored by sacred flame or blessed with incense or kissed at the conclusion of the reading, communicates its significance and worth far more than does a flimsy, newsprint missalette or leaflet.

Sharing of Ministry

What do you think should be done to improve public services in your community: transportation, health care, garbage disposal, etc.

. . . Please try to imagine yourself in this scene:

(1) A musical interlude ending with a crescendo preceded the reading of the word of the Lord. As the crescendo passage began, a minister carried to the celebrant, through the crowd standing around him, a very large (perhaps 26 by 18 inch), handsomely-bound book. He was accompanied by another minister, with smoking censer. The two walked slowly and with measured dignity. When they reached the celebrant, they stood facing him, the celebrant acknowledged them, touched and opened the book with marked deliberateness, found his place and waited calmly. The minister of the book held it in his hands, open toward the celebrant, its top resting on the minister's forehead or chest. The music reached its climax, ceased into a moment of anticipatory silence, and the celebrant began to read.

Now please try to imagine yourself in another scene, this one:

(2) The congregation had barely muttered its "Thanks be to God" after the second reading, when the lector continued rapidly: "Please join in the Alleluia on page ten. Alleluia, Alleluia, Alleluia." After she, like Bob

and Ray, had said her song, her verse, the congregation repeated dully, "Alleluia, Alleluia, Alleluia." The lector retired. The presiding priest shifted forward a foot from his chair, held up one of those little monthly newsprint missalettes, and, without any ceremony at all, read the gospel.

Both are accurate descriptions of recent experiences—fragmentary, but sufficient to make a point. The point is that a great many people who are planning and leading liturgical celebrations these days will spend time choosing a reading, deliberating on the particular translation of the scriptures to be employed, but will not give a thought to the atmosphere created by the action surrounding the reading, the visual and sign value of the way the reading is handled.

The first, of course, was not liturgical. It describes that section of Leonard Bernstein's *Mass: a theatre piece for singers, players and dancers.* . . . The second, of course, was liturgical. It describes that part of a Sunday celebration in a good (in terms of liturgical concern and effort) parish in Washington, D.C. . . .

Robert Hovda[10]

Another non-verbal element is the way ministry is conducted during the liturgy of the word. Whether ministry is monopolized by the ordained minister(s)—in reading all the scripture lessons, preaching, saying the prayers of the community, and so on—or whether the ministry is shared with lay members of the congregation, speaks a message of its own. If the laity are considered disciples who preach and witness to the word in their lives during the week, and if there is indeed a radical equality among the baptized, then this ministerial, equitable lifestyle is appropriately expressed on Sunday through participation in the proclamation of scripture and by preparation and leadership in the prayers of the people. This does not detract from the proper role of the clergy, but clarifies it. For if ordained ministers monopolize all ministry on Sunday, the implication is given that they are to monopolize all ministry during the week as well. And conversely . . .

The ministry of proclaiming the scripture readings may thus be shared by lay persons and clergy. In some churches it is the practice for one or two lay persons to read the first two readings, and for an ordained minister to read the third. The sharing of this ministry by lay women and men, including older children, non-verbally communicates several important messages: for example, that lay persons do have a place in the public ministry of the church, that women, children and men share in public ministry, and that the word belongs to all the baptized and not just to the clergy. In addition, the liturgical reading of scripture by laity should be a reflection of that proclamation of the good news that all—including laity—are doing during the week, and a reminder and example that all should be doing so in their everyday lives.

Then the Memoirs of the Apostles or the Writings of the Prophets are read for as long as time allows. When the reader has finished, the president speaks, exhorting us to live by these noble teachings.

Justin Martyr[11]

What's Happening Now?

Describe the message "preached" by the architectural setting of the liturgy of the word regarding Jesus Christ, regarding the preacher, and regarding the congregation.

To what extent and what ways is the ministry of the word shared by ordained and lay members of your congregation?

Are the Connections Being Made?

How well do the non-verbal dimensions of the liturgy of the word of your own Sunday worship express social justice values? Fail to express them? Contradict them?

Are There Changes To Be Made?

Identify aspects of the non-verbal part of the liturgy of the word that are good and that you want to affirm, support and see continued. How will you support these?

Identify practices that need to be improved, corrected or changed. What alternatives to these practices can you envision? What can you do to bring about these changes?

If You Have Energy For Just One Area, Start Here:

Engage a number of lay persons in the reading of scripture in your liturgies.
or
Rearrange the seating in your church so that a better theological message regarding Christ, the minister, and the people is expressed.

VERBAL DIMENSIONS

In structure, the liturgy of the word consists of three types of verbal elements: the proclamation of the scriptural word, the preaching of the word, and the community's response to the word proclaimed and preached.

Proclaiming the Word

What's a "good news" story you've heard lately?

One, two or three passages from the Bible are proclaimed to the worshiping community. An increasingly common pattern is to read a selection from the Hebrew Bible or Old Testament first (or one from the Acts of the Apostles during the Easter season), one from the epistles of the New Testament or the book of Revelation second, and a passage from one of the Gospels as the third lesson.

The practice of using a lectionary or assigned sequence of readings is to be commended. A lectionary provides a clear and systematic approach to the church year, centered upon the paschal mystery. A lectionary links us to the church catholic, for those common texts are shared by many other communities of faith and in other areas of the world. It can be a catalyst to one's sense of justice and solidarity to know that the texts you hear on a given Sunday are being read as well that day throughout the world in Christ's church. A lectionary also helps in assuring that the word addresses us and that we do not select texts to fit a particular mood or incident. Use of a lectionary also allows the entire assembly to know what particular texts are forthcoming so that they may prepare themselves through study, prayer or family devotions.

The scriptural word needs to be proclaimed well. Preparation leads to better proclamation of the word. Readers, or lectors, with the appropriate skills may be encouraged to practice their readings. It goes without saying that the reading needs to be heard with clarity by all in the assembly.

The reader of the first lesson need not be in too much of a hurry to begin. Let the people be seated, get settled, and prepare themselves to be attentive to the word. It may be helpful to provide a very brief introduction to the readings to aid in setting their context. The text may be announced simply, with reference only to the particular book of the Bible from which it is taken.

But more is required than mere public speaking technique. The use of the term "proclamation" in this context means that the scripture passage has a message which is first of all of great importance to the reader, and which the reader believes is of great importance to all the people; thus the reader's intention will be to communicate this important message to every single person present.

The language that is used will welcome or alienate members of the worshiping community. Concern for all the gathered people requires that care be taken to employ language that is hospitably inclusive. With preparation, readings can be prepared to avoid exclusive, alienating phrases and enlarge them to be more embracing of the entire community. Such inclusive

The first lesson is from the ___ chapter of ___ . Here ends the reading.[12]

A reading from _____ . The word of the Lord.[13]

This is the gospel of the Lord. Praise to you, Lord Jesus Christ.[14]

The gospel of Christ. Praise to you, Lord Jesus Christ.[15]

The gospel of the Lord. Praise to you, O Christ.[16]

Passage. The selection of scripture that is proclaimed is variously called the *lesson, reading,* or *lection.*

The Authors

language will communicate the message with grace and sensitivity.

As mentioned above, the proclamation of the word usually includes readings from the Old Testament as well as the New. The Old Testament proclaims many clear, prophetic statements on God and justice, and it bears the presence of God's word. In addition, the inclusion of Old Testament texts provides a meaningful point of contact for the Church with the Jewish community—those who were first called into covenantal relationship with God and who first bore witness to the one living God. In this century of the holocaust and vibrant anti-semitism, the maintenance and growth of Jewish-Christian relations is important to us all and is a matter of social justice.

On occasion, proclamation may take the form of dramatic rendition, with several readers involved. For example, on the Sunday of the passion, or Palm Sunday, to have a number of readers involved in the proclamation of the passion narrative can bring that familiar story alive with new insight and fresh meaning.

The Lectionary

Today many churches choose the scripture passages to be proclaimed each Sunday according to what is called a "lectionary system," and some read them from a book called a "lectionary" rather than from a Bible.

A lectionary is simply the Bible arranged for proclamation and preaching during worship.

The basic plan of the lectionary most commonly used today in North America is to read virtually all of the New Testament on Sunday during a three year period, together with a substantial portion of the Old Testament or Hebrew Bible.

To do this it lays out three biblical readings for each Sunday, one from the gospels, one from the New Testament epistles (and the book of Revelation), and one from the Old Testament.

In the first year of the three year cycle, the gospel according to Matthew is read in its entirety. The second year then focuses on Mark, and the third year, on Luke. John's gospel is read in part at the end of the second year, because of the brevity of Mark; in addition it is used prominently during the Easter season of all three years.

Two different approaches are used to choose the readings for individual Sundays. The year is divided into two types of Sundays. The first are those of the "seasons," constituting the periods during which we prepare for Christmas (Advent) and Easter (Lent), together with the periods during which we prolong the celebration of these central feasts (the Christmas season, extending to Epiphany or the baptism of the Lord; the Easter season, extending to Pentecost); these seasons include about nineteen Sundays.

Secondly, there are the thirty-three Sundays between the end of the Christmas season and the beginning of Lent, and after Pentecost and before Advent. In different churches these are called "ordinary time," or the "propers," or simply "Sundays after Epiphany" and "Sundays after Pentecost."

The three readings for the Sundays of the seasons are chosen with reference to the meaning of each season; for each Sunday the three readings therefore tend to be related thematically.

During the rest of the year, however, the gospel and epistles are read more or less consecutively—straight through—of course skipping over passages already chosen for the seasons. In this case the gospel and epistle readings are quite independent of each other.

In different churches, two systems govern the choice of Old Testament readings for the Sundays after Pentecost. One is to choose passages that are related thematically to the gospel of the Sunday. The other is simply to read particularly important parts of the Old Testament in a consecutive fashion.

To a very considerable extent the larger churches in North America have accepted the lectionary system described here, though there still are some individual differences from one church to another.

The Authors

Preaching the Word

Following the proclamation of the scriptural word, the word is then preached. Ancient stories of God and Israel, of Jesus and Paul, are brought to contemporary significance in preaching.

The scriptural word needs to be preached well. It should be to, and for, the baptized community, those who are engaged in sharing the good news of Jesus Christ and in preparing for the reign of God in their everyday lives. The preaching has to be for today, leading to the transformation of lives tomorrow. It must balance comfort and challenge in a way that affects the lives of the people. Preaching needs to be addressed not just to individuals, but to individuals-in-community and to the community as a whole. Preaching requires not a monologue, but a dialogue which invites a response.

Earlier comments about word and architecture may be recalled here. Does the pulpit present a barrier between preacher and people? In some smaller worshiping communities, it may be possible for the preacher to stand near or among the community to effectively and non-verbally underscore that the word is addressed to all the baptized, including the preacher.

Preaching is always relevant to social justice, even though it may not on a particular occasion deal with an explicit social justice issue. Conversely, there are a number of ways in which preaching can fail to support social justice values, and even contradict them. Four points that are relevant here are the following:

1. Preaching has a communal dimension, and is not solely addressed to individuals.
2. Preaching is, at least in part, outward looking, leading people beyond themselves, and beyond their own church community. Preaching takes into account that there is a big, hurting world "out there," one to which we are called to minister.
3. Preaching not only looks to eternal life—or to "other-worldly" dimensions—but also attributes importance to this world and this life.
4. Preaching recognizes that the hearers of the word are all called to ministry and discipleship, and that they are active participants in the ministry of the whole church.

Preaching may explicitly address social justice issues, either in passing or as a major theme. As we know, this may result in controversy. More than once, the complaint "Keep out of politics! Stick to the gospel!" has been voiced. Dr. Allan Boesak was once asked how he responded to preachers who

This holy Mass, this Eucharist, is clearly an act of faith. Our Christian faith shows us that in this moment contention is changed into the body of the Lord who offers himself for the redemption of the world. In the chalice the wine is transformed into the blood that is the price of salvation. May this body broken and this blood shed for human beings encourage us to give our body and blood up to suffering and pain, as Christ did—not for self, but to bring justice and peace to our people. Let us be intimately united then in faith and hope. . . .

Oscar Romero

At this point Archbishop Oscar Romero was shot and died.[17]

He died at the altar celebrating mass, a fitting symbol of his life as priest and bishop, a life dedicated to total service to his church and the people of El Salvador. In three years as Archbishop he had become the voice of those who had no voice, the incorruptible defender of the rights of the poor and oppressed, the untiring denouncer of injustice, the hopeful proclaimer of the kingdom of love and trust, and the faithful companion of all those who work for justice and peace.

William Wipfler[18]

Resources

Social Themes of the Christian Year: A Commentary on the Lectionary, edited by D. T. Hessel (Philadelphia: The Geneva Press, 1983)

Liberation Preaching: The Pulpit and the Oppressed, by J. L. Gonzales and C. G. Gonzalez (Nashville: Abingdon 1980)

"Preaching the Just Word" by Walter Burghardt, in Liturgy and Social Justice, edited by M. Searle (Collegeville: Liturgical Press 1980)

Preaching on Peace, edited by R. J. Sider and D. J. Brubaker (Philadelphia: Fortress Press 1982)

declared that the church should stay out of politics. His response was to urge them to go back to the seminary and read the Bible again to see how time and time again God's good news engages the bad news of political powers, whether Pharaoh, Ahab, Herod, Pilate or Caesar. Archbishop Desmond Tutu, like Boesak a South African, has been quoted as saying, "I am confused about which Bible people are talking about when they say that religion and politics don't mix."

Walter Burghardt offers some graceful, yet faithful means of preaching on social justice themes:

1. The preacher is a sinner too. Such an awareness may help to avoid a dogmatic, pulpit pounding barrage. Issues may be raised and explored, informing the assembly where the church and/or the preacher stands, and why.
2. The consciences of the people should be questioned, not coerced. They may be challenged to reflect and examine themselves in light of the gospel. Because the preaching situation is one where the audience is "captive," Burghardt suggests that another forum be provided for active dialogue, open discussion and debate. A study group after the worship or during the week would be one such forum.
3. The preacher need not denigrate or put down the people. Rather s/he will want to encourage, arouse and empower them.
4. Finally, the preacher will be careful to live and celebrate the word that s/he preaches.[19]

Responding to the Word

The basic dynamic of the liturgy of the word is not monologue, but dialogue: proclamation and preaching are balanced by the response of the people. The word of God is spoken to us—as individuals and as community—and seeks, even demands, a response. In its most basic form this response is simply "yes" or "no"; and to ignore the word, or to neglect to respond to it, is really to say "no."

At a private and interior level, we respond personally as the word is proclaimed and preached. At the public and communal level, however, our response is expressed liturgically following the individual scripture readings and preaching. This may be done in a number of ways, which to some extent vary among churches. It is very important in planning and leading worship, however, to be sure that the element of response not be short-changed.

A carefully paced liturgy will encourage the response of the people to the word. In the first place, the liturgy need not be rushed. Secondly, silence may be allowed and recognized as a significant mode of response. Ample periods of silence may follow readings of scripture and/or the sermon to allow individuals to make the communicated message their own.

Communal, verbal, responses then follow. These responses should be engaging and permit not only intellectual, but also bodily, imaginative and affective response. One pattern, used in some churches, is that a psalm, or a portion of one, is used as a response to the first reading, silence after the second, and a hymn after the third reading or following the sermon. In addition, a creed, intercessions—"prayer of the church" or "general intercession" or "prayer of the faithful"—and the offering or collection are additional modes of response.

The Psalm

In what ways is the voice of the poor and marginalized expressed and heard in your society?

What feelings of solidarity are there between your community and those who are seeking peace, freedom, and justice in Central America, South Korea, Lebanon, and elsewhere?

The psalms are not to be thought of as merely pious religious poetry inserted into the liturgy to fill a gap, or to provide an opportunity for congregational participation; nor are they an additional scripture reading. Instead, the psalms provide an opportunity to enter into some of the deepest and most moving religious expression of our tradition. Used liturgically by the people of Israel and throughout Christian history as well, the psalms have considerable relevance as well to our theme of social justice.

Many of the psalms speak about life the way it really is; they speak about human experience very honestly. If there is pain and grief, if life is not good, then dismay and anger are expressed openly. This may serve to open our own eyes and shatter our own complacency; it lets us hear the voices of those in pain around the world; it invites us to join in solidarity with them; it urges us to refuse to settle for things as they are; it calls us to a response of ministry both to heal the wounded and to remove wounding situations.

The psalms also assert very strongly that only God is God. They remind us that our God has delivered before, continues to deliver, and that we respond in thanksgiving and praise. We proclaim that our God is the creator, and that God continues to create. We proclaim that our God rules, and that this rule provides a model of justice, love and concern for the poor.

Sharing and Witnessing

The assembly's response to preaching might include a time

Be gracious to me, O God, for the enemy
  persecutes me;
my adversaries harass me all day long.
All day long my watchful foes persecute me;
countless are those who oppress me.
Appear on high in my day of fear.
I put my trust in you.
With God to help me I will stand firm.
In God I trust, and I shall not be afraid.
What can mortals do to me?
All day long they plot to harm me;
all their thoughts are hostile.
They are on the lookout;
they conspire and spy on my footsteps.
But while they lie in wait for me,
it is they who will not escape.
O God, in your anger bring ruin on the
  nations.
Enter my lament in your book;
store every tear in your flask.
Then my enemies will be turned back
on the day when I call upon you;
for this I know—that God is with me.
In God I trust and shall not be afraid.
What can mortals do to me?
I have bound myself with vows to you, O
  God,
and will fulfill them with thank offerings;
for you have rescued me from death—
to walk in your presence, in the light of life.

Psalm 56

A Modern Creed: United Church of Canada

We are not alone, we live in God's world.
We believe in God:
who has created and is creating,
who has come in Jesus, the Word made flesh,
to reconcile and make new,
who works in us and others by the Spirit.

We trust in God.

We are called to be the Chruch:
to celebrate God's presence,
to love and serve others,
to seek justice and resist evil,
to proclaim Jesus, crucified and risen,
our judge and our hope.

In life, in death, in life beyond death,
God is with us.
We are not alone. Thanks be to God.

of sharing among members of the congregation, in pairs, in small groups, or in dialogue with the preacher. In some churches, particularly in Latin America and Africa, there is the custom of people being invited to speak about, or witness, how the texts have influenced their lives. *The Gospel at Solentiname* is the title of a multi-volume series of books that records the reflections and observations of a group of Nicaraguan peasants. These simple, uneducated villagers share their comments and insights into the gospel lesson that is read. Their observations and reflections are profound and meaningful. They offer an excellent illustration of the communal benefit that may be gained by sharing and conversing within the worshiping assembly.

The Creed

The creed, or profession of faith, is a response in which the individual's voice is joined to that of the community. The traditional Apostles' or Nicene Creed is employed in some churches, while others use more contemporary compositions. The Apostles' Creed, which dates from the early centuries of the church, is the profession of faith of our baptism and bears with it a baptismal emphasis as it begins, "I believe. . . ." The Nicene Creed, which dates from the fourth century, is the corporate creed of the church, a strong declaration in the face of heretical threats, and thus begins, "We believe. . . ." With both creeds, their intention is to provide a corporate response to the assembly's encounter with the living Christ in God's word, to declare explicitly the source and focus of our faith. As such, there is implicit in the creeds a correction against idolatry as the community reaffirms its faith in the one, living, triune God.

Prayers of Intercession

The word invites a response of concern and prayer for the needs of the world. These prayers need to be concrete and specific, relevant to the world and to the people present. They are of worldwide scope and prayed with feeling. Such prayers will demonstrate a balance between particular and universal needs, between concerns associated with people we name and those who cannot be named.

The prayers are one of the clearest points where worship and social justice are brought together. It is as if the windows of the sanctuary are thrown open and the cries of the wounded, broken world are heard. With painful awareness of the injustice and oppression in the world, of exploited people and environment, of the seeming reign of death in this era of the fall, we gather together to pray to God for God's intervention, for the saving presence of God or for God's healing Spirit. To demonstrate the variety of ministries, these prayers are prepared and led by lay members of the community. Or a time of silence

General Intercessions

(Prayers of the Faithful, Prayers of the People, Prayers of the Church)

These prayers, though appropriately (but briefly) introduced and concluded by the presiding minister, should come from the people and not be usurped by the minister.

While some of the prayers typically will be prepared by a group or individual, it is preferable that there also be an invitation to the congregation at large to add other, spontaneous, intentions as well. Having only spontaneous prayers often leads to prayers that are narrow, and not always well thought out. Having only prepared prayers may neglect needs that are present in the assembly.

In these prayers all pray for needs or intentions of which they have become aware through their ministerial lives during the week, through the word of God they have just experienced, and through their vision of the reign of God.

The traditional "classes" of intentions are (a) the needs of the church, (b) civil society and the world at large, (c) those oppressed by any need, (d) the local community, and (e) special occasions or special categories of people.

These prayers should take the worshiping assembly beyond itself, and should express its real concern for others; they should be caring and even "passionate." Intentions that are too narrow or trivial are inappropriate. It is best, therefore, that they be composed each week in the local community; those taken from books, or composed elsewhere, usually are not entirely appropriate, though they can provide very useful ideas.

Prayers for the church may (on different days) refer to the church in different countries and regions of the world; in different regions in our own country; different ministries; different categories of church members; the ecumenical church and Christian unity; heroes and heroines of the church, etc.

Prayers for civil society, the world at large, those oppressed, and for the local community often are appropriately inspired by Saturday or Sunday newspapers or news broadcasts, and by the personal experience and knowledge of members of the community.

These prayers may be expressed in several different styles.

One form is (a) an invitation to pray for an area of concern (e.g., let us pray for the children of the world); (b) a period of silent prayer, and (c) a concluding short vocal prayer which attempts to sum up the silent prayers of all.

A second form is a brief prayer by the leader, followed by a congregational response. This may take the form of "let us pray for/that . . . ; let us remember . . . ; for all . . . ; that . . . ; for. . . .

These intentions usually lead to a concluding formula, such as: "we pray to the Lord; we pray to you; O Lord, we trust in you, our God; our hope is in you, O Lord; Lord, in your mercy," etc.

A community response then follows, such as "hear our prayer; Lord, hear our prayer; Lord, have mercy; for you have done great things for us; for you bring us life," etc.

The Authors

---

may be offered for specific intercessions to be voiced by the gathered people themselves.

As in all prayer, it is well to remember that while the prayers are addressed to God, we are or may become God's instruments in meeting the needs we name. The prayers will sensitize us and make us aware of our own ability and responsibility in responding to the concerns named. To pray for justice is to move us to act for justice in our ministries and lives.

Offering or Collection

Do you know how much of your tax dollar is allocated for military expenditures?

How much foreign aid does your government give? What restrictions or strings are placed on this aid? Should more be given?

Is your system of taxation compassionate to those with low incomes?

Intercessory prayers "are not recommendations to God as to how He should behave in the world; on the contrary, they are my commitment for the world before God, my surrender to God and my adoption by God into His service."

Vilmos Vajta[20]

Offering. While some churches refer to the money donated by the members of the assembly as the *offering,* others always use the term *collection.* We use both terms interchangeably.

The Authors

Once there was a church
    where the people took the offering back
        home with them.
First it was collected and brought to the
    altar.
After they asked God to bless it,
    they put it back into their pockets.
    They mixed it up with all their other
        money,
    So that they couldn't tell which was
        blessed and which was not.
Then they left.
All week they spent as though each piece
    was blessed.
And was to be used lovingly.

Herbert Brokering[21]

And all who believed were together and had all things in common; and they sold their possessions and goods and distributed them to all, as any had need.

Acts 2:44–45

In the third century, the North African bishop, Cyprian, wrote once to reprimand a wealthy woman in his church who made no offering of her resources for the care of the poor but who presumed nevertheless to show up at the communion table. From Cyprian's perspective, the poor and rich alike must spend themselves for others. This is the concrete self-gift of the church, the gift celebrated in the eucharist. The wealthy woman who refused her gift was denying—even mocking—the trust of the eucharist. The eucharist is, above all else, a sacrifice: yours—joined to Christ's.

Mary Collins[22]

The word leads us to profession of faith, to prayer, and finally to action. This can and should begin with "the offering" or "the collection," which is another key juncture of worship and social justice. In the early church, we are told that the believers *had all things in common; and they sold their possessions and goods and distributed them to all, as any had need* (Acts 2:44–45). Justin Martyr, writing around the year 150, reported that the liturgical president, in addition to preaching and praying at the eucharist, administered the collection. These monies were used for acts of justice and mercy; they were part of the assembly's ministry in the world. The offering was used to assist orphans and widows, those in want through sickness or unemployment, those who were hungry or imprisoned, refugees, sojourners, all who were in need.

Today our monies do the same, although increasing amounts have gone to maintenance of the institutional church or to buildings which house the church, the people of God. The collection needs to be seen not merely as a means to pay the bills or the minister, but clearly in relation to the prayers. Our offerings, because they bear our prayers, are related to social justice; they need to be generous, ample, and sacrificial. People will welcome the opportunity to be informed of how the money collected is spent, to be aware that part of the money is going to assist those who are in any need. The congregation deserves the assurance that the collection is used with good stewardship, accountability, and with justice and mercy.

When the eucharist is celebrated, the procession that brings up the offering may also present the gifts of bread and wine. The collection thereby becomes part of the "setting the table" phase of the liturgy of the eucharist as well as part of the "response" phase of the liturgy of the word.

In some churches it is the custom to accompany the presentation of the offering with the singing of the "doxology." The traditional text for this is:

> Praise God from whom all blessings flow,
> Praise Him all creatures here below,
> Praise Him above the heavenly host,
> Praise Father, Son and Holy Ghost.

Many congregations are experimenting with new versions in order to express a wider range of images of God, as well as to express other theological concepts besides "heaven above" and "here below."

Sign of Peace and Confession

In some churches other forms of response to the Word proclaimed and preached are also celebrated. Thus the "confession" sometimes follows the word rather than be part of the gathering liturgy. This may be especially appropriate during Lent.

In addition, following ancient precedent, some churches exchange the sign of peace at the end of the liturgy of the word, as the community prepares to bring its gifts to the altar. This certainly is as appropriate an occasion on which to pray Christ's peace for each other as the other customary position, prior to communion.

What's Happening Now?

When you listen to the word of God proclaimed, what kinds of thoughts and emotions have you experienced?

How has the preaching of the word led you further into ministry and discipleship and linked you in solidarity with others around the world?

After listening to the preaching, how would you like to respond during worship? For example, through silence and a brief sharing with one or two around you? Sharing in small groups? Other ways? What do you think would strengthen and enlighten your worship community?

What balance is there between the proclamation and preaching of the word, and of congregational response to the word? What priority does congregational response to the word have for your minister? (Or, if you are the minister, what priority does congregational response have for you?)

Are The Connections Being Made?

How well do the verbal dimensions of the liturgy of the word of your own Sunday worship express social justice values? Fail to express them? Contradict them?

Are There Changes To Be Made?

Identify aspects of the verbal dimensions of the liturgy of the word that you want to affirm, support and see continued. How will you support these?

Identify practices that need to be improved, corrected or changed. What alternatives to these practices can you envision? What can you do to bring about these changes?

If You Have Energy For Just One Area, Start Here:

Experiment (carefully) with a congregational response to the preaching of the word that is different from your present practice.

6. The Liturgy of Baptism

Introduction

Baptism and Social Justice

    The God We Worship
        Baptism proclaims that only God is God
        Baptism is a participation in Christ's death and resurrection
        Baptism is a gift of the Holy Spirit
        Baptism is a sign of God's reign

    The People Who Worship
        Baptism is incorporation into the body of Christ
        Baptism makes us part of a community, a family
        Baptism identifies us as new creatures, heirs to God's reign

    Our Mission and Ministry
        Baptism is a conversion, pardoning, and cleansing
        Baptism marks the beginning of a lifestyle of faith that witnesses to the reign of God
        Baptism sends the people of God into the world in mission, witness and service

The Liturgical Celebration

    Non-Verbal Dimensions
        Preparation
        Time
        Place
        Sharing of ministry
        Architecture
        Water

    Verbal Dimensions
        Immediate preparation for baptism
           Dialogue with the minister

76

Prayers and instructions
Prayer over the water
Profession of faith and baptism
Welcoming the newly baptized
Laying on of hands and signing with the cross
Oil or chrism
White garment
Lighted candle

The word proclaimed and preached calls women and men to faith and discipleship, and it is therefore fitting that baptism be celebrated immediately following the liturgy of the word.

The core of the liturgy of baptism consists of the profession of faith and the baptism itself: the immersion or pouring of water in the name of the Father, Son and Holy Spirit.

Before these central elements, however, there are other prayers and actions which help to express the meaning of baptism and declare the commitment of the candidates or their parents and sponsors. After the baptism proper, other prayers and actions welcome the candidates into the community. The parts of the liturgy of baptism that precede and follow the core of the liturgy vary somewhat from church to church.

What Is Your Own Experience?

Think about your own experience of the liturgy of baptism when it is celebrated within Sunday worship. Does this have meaning for you?

Describe what actually happens when a baptism is celebrated during the Sunday liturgy.

Baptism and Social Justice

How might you describe your understanding of baptism? In what ways, if at all, is baptism related to social justice? Again, the wisdom of the church sets before us a strong and compelling vision of the relationship between social justice and the liturgy of baptism.

Baptism is the sacrament of new life in Jesus Christ uniting one with Christ and incorporating one into Christ's body, the church. One church's liturgy for holy baptism summarizes the meaning of baptism this way:

> In Holy Baptism our gracious heavenly Father liberates us from sin and death by joining us to the death and resurrection of our Lord Jesus Christ. We are born children of a fallen humanity; in the waters of Baptism we are reborn children of God and inheritors of eternal life. By water and the Holy Spirit we are made members of the Church which is the body of Christ. As we live with him and with his people, we grow in faith, love, and obedience to the will of God.[1]

Baptism declares who our God is, who we are, and what mission and ministry is entrusted to us.

The God We Worship

Baptism Proclaims that Only God Is God

We baptize, and are baptized, in the name of the triune God, thus naming the one true God whose child we become. First, however, we renounce sin and evil and all that is not God and against God, and profess our faith in the same triune God.

Baptism Is a Participation in Christ's Death and Resurrection

Death and life imagery is indelibly etched into the Christian understanding of baptism. In Romans, Paul writes about dying with Christ, being baptized into Christ's death, being buried with Christ. In Mark's gospel, when James and John ask Jesus for special places in the kingdom, Jesus responds: *Are you able . . . to be baptized with the baptism with which I am baptized?* (Mark 10:38). He of course refers to his death.

Yet as Jesus' death was the threshold to life, so in baptism there is a movement from death to life. We are buried with Christ in baptism so that as Christ was raised so shall we be raised. Our baptismal drowning is the prelude to new life. We become a new creation, new creatures.

> Do you not know that all of us who have been baptized into Christ Jesus were baptized into his death? We were buried therefore with him by baptism into death, so that as Christ was raised from the dead by the glory of the Father, we too might walk in newness of life.
>
> For if we have been united with him in a death like his, we shall certainly be united with him in a resurrection like his. We know that our old self was crucified with him so that the sinful body might be destroyed, and we might no longer be enslaved to sin. For he who has died is freed from sin. But if we have died with Christ, we believe that we shall also live with him. For we know that Christ being raised from the dead will never die again; death no longer has dominion over him. The death he died he died to sin, once for all, but the life he lives he lives to God. So you also must consider yourselves dead to sin and alive to God in Christ Jesus.
>
> Romans 6:1–11

> In the beginning God created the heavens and the earth. Now the earth was a formless void, there was darkness over the deep, and God's spirit hovered over the water.
>
> Genesis 1:1–2

78

In the fullness of time,
you sent your only Son to save us.
Incarnate by the Holy Spirit,
born of your favoured one, Mary,
sharing our life, he reconciled us to your love,
At the Jordan your Spirit descended upon
    him,
anointing him to preach the good news of
    your reign.
He healed the sick and fed the hungry,
manifesting the power of your compassion.
He sought out the lost and broke bread with
    sinners,
witnessing the fullness of your grace.
We beheld his glory.[2]

Baptism Is a Gift of the Holy Spirit

God's Spirit embraces all of life; the Spirit is involved before, during and following our baptism. This is the Spirit that brooded over the waters at creation; the Spirit that was breathed into and enlivened humanity; the Spirit that animated Ezekiel's vision of dry bones; the Spirit that descended upon Jesus at his baptism in the Jordan; the Spirit invoked by Jesus at Nazareth, who anointed him to bring good news to the poor, the blind, captive and the oppressed; the Spirit of Pentecost that united and empowered the church. In baptism we are anointed and sealed by the Holy Spirit. This Spirit continues as our lifelong companion, nurturing our faith, empowering our lives and animating our prayer.

Baptism Is a Sign of God's Reign

John's ministry of baptism pointed to the reign of God being at hand. Jesus' public ministry began after his baptism, a ministry that incarnated the kingdom. In similar fashion our baptism is a sign of the reign of God. We become "kingdom people," initiated through the Church into the new life of the kingdom. In our baptismal commission to ministry we become witnesses to the reign of God.

The People Who Worship

Baptism Is Incorporation into the Body of Christ

The baptismal font has sometimes been referred to as the womb of the church. All Christians are born again, initiated by baptism into the body of Christ, the church. We thus share a baptismal bond of unity with Christ and with the church catholic—all who ever have named, or will name, the name of Jesus and serve Christ as his disciples extending his ministry to all the earth.

This baptismal bond of unity links us with all of our sisters and brothers in Christ. We are joined across the centuries of time, united beyond the bounds of geography and political borders, and gathered into *koinonia*—fellowship, community, communion—of all Christian churches which otherwise seem so fragmented and divided. Baptism bridges our human division and calls us to the essential unity of *one body, one Spirit, one hope, one Lord, one faith, one baptism, one God. . . .*

Baptism Makes Us Part of a Community, a Family

New Testament images of baptism as a rebirth or adoption imply incorporation into a family. Indeed, as with our birth into our human family, in baptism we are named when we become a part of the family of God. This new identity as a child, one among the children of God, gifts us with a community orientation. Self-centered individualism is diminished as we share in the community's life. We are further gifted in baptism with a sense of joy and hope, for we have become a part of God's family. And as St. Paul declares, nothing—not principalities or powers, not even death—nothing can separate us from the love of God in Christ Jesus our Lord.

Baptism Identifies Us as New Creatures, Heirs to God's Reign

As St. Paul reminds us, within the body of Christ, social barriers of the world are washed away: we are no longer male nor female, slave nor free, Jew nor Greek, but all one, sisters and brothers in Christ. A radical equality and unity is thus effected within the baptized community as we are called away from conformity and toward transformation. Brazilian Archbishop Dom Helder Camara incarnated this sense of transformation when he spoke out repeatedly *in pastoral defense of human dignity.* Such a defense underscores the radical equality of the baptized community. All are equal, new creatures, beloved heirs to God's reign.

It is precisely this radical equality and unity, for example, that makes South African apartheid a theological heresy. Apartheid began in the last century in the Dutch Reformed Church of South Africa when white people decided that black people should not be baptized in, nor attend, the same churches as whites. Blacks were relegated to their own congregations within the Dutch Reformed system. After World War II, with the election of the Nationalist Party, what began as a church system of separation of races became official government policy. Baptism directly confronts the demonic system of apartheid, exposing its essential evil in separating people whom God has joined together in the family of God.

Our Mission and Ministry

Baptism Is a Conversion, Pardoning, and Cleansing

In baptism, the old person is drowned, put to death, and a new person arises. John the Baptist spoke of this transformation is terms of repentance, *metanoia.* Metanoia literally means *to turn around,* to reorient and recenter oneself around Christ.

This baptized new person is liberated from sin and death, pardoned and cleansed. Baptismal imagery of rebirth, new life, being born again, emphasizes the new beginnings associated with baptism. We are set free to serve Christ in obedience.

Baptism thus has ethical implications. Through our conversion and pardoning we are called to turn away from our old life, to leave behind one set of values and embrace another, Christian way of living. One is called to *put on the mind of Christ,* to put to death what is earthly and put on the attributes

There is one body and one Spirit, just as you were called to the one hope that belongs to your call; one Lord, one faith, one baptism, one God and Father of us all, who is above all and through all and in all.

Ephesians 4:4–6

Where else in our society are all of us—not just a gnostic elite, but everyone—called to be social critics, called to extricate ourselves from the powers and principalities that claim to rule our daily lives, in order to submit ourselves to the sole dominion of the God before whom all of us are equal? Where else in our society are we all addressed and sprinkled and bowed to and incensed and touched and kissed and treated like *somebody*—all in the very same way? Where else do economic czars and beggars get the same treatment? Where else are food and drink blessed in a common prayer of thanksgiving, broken and poured out, so that everybody, everybody shares and shares alike?

Robert W. Hovda[3]

And the multitudes asked him, "What then shall we do?" And he answered them, "He who has two coats, let him share with him who has none; and he who has food, let him do likewise." Tax collectors also came to be baptized, and said to him, "Teacher, what shall we do?" And he said to them, "Collect no more than is appointed you. Soldiers also asked him, "And we, what shall we do?" And he said to them, "Rob no one by violence or by false accusation, and be content with your wages."

Luke 3:10–14

Walk Humbly

Walk humbly my people, embrace one
   another
Sing softly your praises in stillness discover,
Creation is crying, faint hearts are dying,
Reach out your arms and gather them in.

Walk gently my people, through fields of the
   weeping,
Press heart to heart, in tenderness keeping,
My love for my children as one with your
   own,
Whisper my hope for forgiveness of sin.

Walk healing my people, midst crowds of
   the needing,
Caressing the weary in sacrifice feeding,
That body and spirit by your nuture
   growing,
Will find deeper meaning and know they
   belong.

Walk boldly my people, your pilgrimage
   sharing,
I journey beside you, my strength and my
   caring
As part of your being my spirit made whole,
Be my hands and my feet and my mouth
   and my song.

Ralph Freeman[5]

of the kingdom. We are called to turn away from greed, violence and injustice and toward the attributes of God's reign: peace, justice, patience, forgiveness, sharing of goods and property, hospitality and equality.

Baptism Marks the Beginning of a Lifestyle of Faith that Witnesses to the Reign of God

A baptismal lifestyle is one which knows, as T. S. Eliot put it, *"the moment of tension between dying and birth."*[4] Those moments of tension are lived out in daily repentance, participation in God's reign, prayer, worship and commitment to justice and peace. Moments of tension between dying and birth point to our baptismal death and our awaiting of physical death when we shall be born to eternal life. In Luke, we encounter John the Baptist's instructions on a baptismal lifestyle: sharing of clothing and food, equitable collection of taxes, prohibition of robbery by violence. In the early church instructions from bishops to the newly baptized called for regular participation in the sacraments of the church, prayer and worship, but also went on to urge acts of mercy and commitment to God's reign of peace and justice.

Micah could be said to have articulated a baptismal lifestyle: *And what does the Lord require of you but to do justice, and to love kindness, and to walk humbly with your God?* (Micah 6:8).

In the early records of the church there is evidence that such lifestyle commitments made by the newly baptized ruled out certain careers or employments; these were deemed incompatible with being baptized. For example, the military, which required oaths of allegiance to a Caesar who considered himself a god; work within a pagan governmental system; and acting, because of its overt sexual immorality. Such occupational transformation was indicative of the ethical demands placed upon the baptized community to live out their faith in daily life. Such historic examples raise for our age similar questions: Should a baptized person work in the nuclear arms industry, or in the employ of the South African government, or in the military, or . . . ? What are the occupational implications of living out our baptismal faith?

Baptism Sends the People of God into the World in Mission, Witness and Service

Sustained and empowered by the Spirit, we are sent forth in ministry, as witnesses to the good news of Christ, as harbingers of God's kingdom and as servants of Christ. The baptized are disciples of Christ, concerned about the world for which Christ died. As Dietrich Bonhoeffer reminds us, this discipleship is costly, for we are called to give our lives in this service, witness and mission.

Reflect On This Vision

Our vision of the relationship between the liturgy of baptism and social justice may be summarized as follows:

The God We Worship
> Baptism proclaims that only God is God
> Baptism is a participation in Christ's death and resurrection
> Baptism is a gift of the Holy Spirit
> Baptism is a sign of God's reign

The People Who Worship
> Baptism is incorporation into the body of Christ
> Baptism makes us part of a community, a family
> Baptism identifies us as new creatures, heirs to God's reign

Our Mission and Ministry
> Baptism is a conversion, pardoning, and cleansing
> Baptism marks the beginning of a lifestyle of faith that witnesses to the reign of God
> Baptism sends the people of God into the world in mission, witness and service

For as many of you as were baptized into Christ have put on Christ. There is neither Jew nor Greek, there is neither slave nor free, there is neither male nor female; for you are all one in Christ Jesus.

Galatians 3:27–28

In what respects does this vision agree with and affirm your own previous understanding of the connection between Sunday worship and social justice?

What ideas regarding this relationship are new to you? How do you react to them?

Participation in Christ's Death and Resurrection

Baptism means participating in the life, death and resurrection of Jesus Christ. Jesus went down into the river Jordan and was baptized in solidarity with sinners in order to fulfil all righteousness (Matt. 3:15). This baptism led Jesus along the way of the Suffering Servant, made manifest in his sufferings, death and resurrection (Mark 10: 38–40). By baptism, Christians are immersed in the liberating death of Christ where their sins are buried, where the "old Adam" is crucified with Christ, and where the power of sin is broken. Thus those baptized are no longer slaves to sin, but free. Fully identified with the death of Christ, they are buried with him and are raised here and now to a new life in the power of the resurrection of Jesus Christ, confident that they will also ultimately be one with him in a resurrection like his (Rom. 5:3–11; Col. 2: 13, 3:1; Eph. 2:5–6).

Baptism, Eucharist, and Ministry[6]

The Liturgical Celebration

Many individual elements of the liturgy of baptism express, work out and implement the vision of the relationship between social justice and baptism that has been enunciated above. We therefore need to consider these one by one.

In addition, we may ask to what extent the vision of the church's best experience and wisdom regarding the liturgy of baptism coincides with our actual experience of baptism on Sunday morning? Because this almost certainly is less than ideal, we need also to ask: How can we change our actual practice so that vision and experience are in greater agreement? How can we improve our liturgical celebration on those occasions when we baptize adults or children on Sunday?

One thing to remember, for example, is that the baptism of a new member of the church—a new sister or brother in Christ—is a significant event not only in the life of the candidate, but also for the whole community. Care, therefore, needs to be taken to make baptism a personal liturgical experience for all present.

NON-VERBAL DIMENSIONS

The first area of possible improvement to examine is that of the non-verbal dimensions of the liturgy of baptism. Though in fact the liturgy of baptism is highly non-verbal throughout, at this point we will consider only the questions of preparation, time, place, architecture, water, and ministry.

Preparation

Do you think there are any occupations which are in basic conflict with the call to follow Christ?

Today, increasing emphasis is being put on the preparation of adult candidates for baptism, and of the preparation of parents and sponsors (godparents) of children who are to be baptized. In the case of older children and adults, many churches precede baptism with an extended period of instruction and formation called the catechumenate. This period is an occasion for the whole community to be involved in teaching and spiritual formation, in leading exemplary lives of faithfulness and witness, in regular prayer for the catechumens.

This practice was the norm in the early centuries of the church. In that age, the church was extremely careful about admitting new members. The catechumenate provided up to three years of instruction, with prayer, repentance and fasting. During this period, the catechumens were excused, with prayer,

Those who are to be initiated into the new faith must first be brought to the catechists to hear the word, before the people arrive.

They are to be asked their reasons for seeking the faith.

Those who introduce them will bear witness in their regard in order that it may be known whether they are capable of hearing the Word. Their state of life also is to be scrutinised.

Enquiry is to be made about the trades and professions of those who are brought for instruction.

If a man is a procurer, that is to say, supports prostitutes, let him give it up or be sent away.

If he is a sculptor or painter, he is to be instructed not to make any more idols. Let him give it up or be sent away.

If he is an actor or gives performances in the theatre, let him give it up or be sent away. [The theatre was associated with sexual immorality.]

If he teaches children, it is preferable that he should give it up. But if he has no trade, he is to be allowed to continue. [Teachers were charged with explaining the primacy of the pagan gods to their pupils.]

If he is a charioteer, a wrestler or attends wrestling matches, let him give it up or be sent away.

If he is gladiator, or teaches gladiators to fight, or a hunter, or if he is a public official who organizes the gladiatorial games, let him give it up or be sent away.

If he is a priest of idols or a guardian of idols, let him give it up or be sent away.

A soldier who is in a position of authority is not to be allowed to put anyone to death; if he is ordered to, he is not to do it, he is not to be allowed to take an oath. If he does not accept these conditions, he is to be sent away.

A man who has the power of the sword, or magistrate of a city who wears the purple; let him give it up or be sent away.

Catechumens or believers who want to enlist as soldiers are to be sent away, for they have treated God with contempt.

A prostitute, or a pederast, or a man who has mutilated himself, or one who has committed the unspeakable thing, are to be sent away, for they are defiled.

Wizards too are not to be admitted as candidates.

Sorcerers, astrologers, fortune-tellers, interpreters of dreams, coiners, makers of amulets must give up these activities; otherwise they are to be sent away.

If a concubine who is the slave of some man has brought up her children and is living only with this man, she is to be admitted; otherwise she is to be sent away.

A man who has a concubine is to give her up and take a wife according to the law. If he refuses he is to be sent away.

If we have omitted anything, make a suitable decision yourselves. For we all have the Spirit of God.

Hippolytus of Rome[7]

---

from worship after the sermon. Only after baptism were they admitted to the church's mysteries: eucharist and the Lord's Prayer.

Our age has been called post-Christian: the era of Christendom has waned and one no longer presumes a Christian culture or society. It is an age in which many believe careful preparation is once again needed to prepare people for baptism, a process which may occasion a renewal of the church. The Baptism, Eucharist, and Ministry document puts it like this: *. . . those [churches] who practice infant baptism . . . must guard themselves against indiscriminate baptism and take more seriously their responsibility for the nurture of baptized children to mature commitment to Christ.* Such initiatives as the Roman Catholic *Rite of Christian Initiation of Adults* are evidence of this shift in awareness and are being experienced as a significant source of renewal in many parishes.

In a post-Christian age, baptism can be a radical event in calling the church to its origins and purpose. As the church carefully prepares and nurtures those people preparing for baptism, the baptized community itself is renewed in its understanding of faithfulness, ministry, and commitment to the reign of God. Such renewal underscores the cost involved in

84

discipleship. For such contemporary figures as Dietrich Bonhoeffer, Martin Luther King, Jr., Ita Ford, and Oscar Romero remind us that the age of martyrs is far from over. To be baptized, to take up one's cross and follow Christ, may put one at cross-purposes (so to speak) with the world.

Time

Do you think there should be a common day of rest for the majority of people?

Within the church year, the privileged time for baptism is at Easter. As the principal annual commemoration and celebration of the death and resurrection of Jesus Christ, it is the most appropriate occasion on which to enact this paschal mystery.

Throughout the rest of the year, some churches encourage baptisms on other especially important and relevant feasts, such as Pentecost, All Saints, and the baptism of our Lord. Some communities may, in addition, feel the need to celebrate baptism more often, even monthly.

Within the week, Sunday is very definitely the most fitting day on which normally to celebrate baptism. The Lord's day after all is the day of Christ's resurrection, the eighth day of creation inaugurating the new age. Sunday is also the day of Pentecost and the beginning of the church through the action of the Holy Spirit.

The Easter Vigil

Perhaps the finest, most appropriate worship setting for baptism is the Easter vigil. This service, held on Holy Saturday night, was *the* occasion for baptism in the early church. As the church gathered in remembrance of Jesus' passage from death to life, the catechumenate shared in that passage through baptism.

The Easter vigil today has a fourfold structure: the service of light, the service of readings, the service of baptism, and the service of eucharist.

The vigil begins at night with the blessing of new fire, the lighting of a large paschal candle, and procession into the body of the church, darkened since Good Friday. As light is shared from paschal candle to hand-held tapers, a cantor sings "The Exsultet," a joyous announcement of the resurrection. This ancient hymn of praise is abundant in its rich themes of remembrance. "This is the night . . ." is a recurrent phrase linking this Holy Saturday night to passover and exodus, resurrection, the triumph of grace and life over sin and death.

Then the service of readings proceeds. Numerous texts are read that are full of baptismal imagery, of life over death: creation, flood, the sacrifice of Isaac, the passover meal, exodus, and the three young men in the fiery furnace are among the lessons read in many churches.

The readings yield to the service of baptism. The prayer over the water again lifts up the baptismal, watery themes of the readings. Baptisms are done, or baptismal covenants reaffirmed.

Then as lights are fully illumined to wash over the assembly, the first eucharist of Easter is joyously celebrated.

The Easter vigil is a powerful liturgical experience because of the lavish biblical richness of word and liturgy, of spoken story and silent ritual. But there is a more subtle element that enhances its power. For the vigil is held at night, in the dark, near the ancient midnight hour of crisis, and not in the garish light of dawn.

The Authors

Place

What is being done to provide sufficient public parks and recreational facilities in all parts of your city or town?

Baptisms should occur in public worship in the midst of the community of God's people. If one dimension of baptism is incorporation into the church, then this should be symbolized and authenticated by celebrating it in the midst of the local church. For the local community is itself a symbol of the reign of God and is the community of disciples among whom the newly baptized will live and grow in faith. The community's role in baptism—pledging its faithful support and welcoming their new brothers and sisters in Christ—is affirmed. Indeed baptisms in public worship afford the entire assembly an occasion to renew and reaffirm their own baptismal covenant and relationship. Private baptisms, whether in homes or church building, are to be avoided.

Sharing of Ministry

Baptism is a celebration of the entire community, and ministry within the liturgy of baptism is to be shared. Parents and sponsors (godparents) of children play special roles, both in worship and in life, raising the children by example and by instruction to realize the fruits of their baptism in lives of faith and ministry. Assisting ministers may be involved in the liturgy to pour water, splashing audibly, from a pitcher into the font before or during the prayer blessing the baptismal waters, or to hold baptismal candles, garments or oil. Children may be involved, and thereby affirmed as members of the community, by inviting them to gather near the font to enable their visual participation.

Architecture

The place of baptism, whether font or pool, should be visible and accessible to the community rather than situated in an out of the way location. In any case, the act of baptism needs to be seen and heard by the entire community. Thus the community may also gather around the font, or they should at least be able to see and hear from their regular seating, or the font may be moved to the front so that all can participate better.

If prominently positioned, the font becomes visible and accessible at all occasions of worship, and a tangible reminder to the community of the centrality of baptism. Some congre-

Incorporation into the Body of Christ

Administered in obedience to our Lord, baptism is a sign and seal of our common discipleship. Through baptism, Christians are brought into union with Christ, with each other and with the Church of every time and place. Our common baptism, which unites us to Christ in faith, is thus a basic bond of unity. We are one people and are called to confess and serve one Lord in each place and in all the world. The union with Christ which we share through baptism has important implications for Christian unity. "There is . . . one baptism, one God and Father of us all . . ." (Eph. 4:4–6). When baptismal unity is realized in one holy, catholic apostolic church, a genuine Christian witness can be made to the healing and reconciling love of God. Therefore, our one baptism into Christ constitutes a call to the churches to overcome their divisions and visibly manifest their fellowship.

Baptism, Eucharist, and Ministry[8]

At a Sunday liturgy where five children of various ages were to be baptized, the minister invited all of the children of the congregation to gather around the font. He explained the symbols of water and fire and then asked for volunteers to receive the baptismal candles and give them to the newly baptized at the appropriate time. One family who were presenting two of their children to be baptized asked their oldest child (already baptized) to speak the names of her brothers. This gave her a special role on a day that was special for her family.

Garneau United Church, Edmonton

In a large parish with an active RCIA (Rite of Christian Initiation of Adults) program, one mother introduces her children to each of the candidates for baptism. This enables the child to feel significant, to make contact with individuals in a sea of adults and to take an active role in welcoming the adult into the worship community. It also works the other way for the adult: feeling included in the parish family, having individual contact within a large worship community and having her or his journey of faith affirmed by the littlest ones of the community.

Joan Halmo[9]

gations place the font at the entrance of the nave as a clear reminder each time one enters the church that it was by baptism that one initially entered the community of the faithful. For example, Westminster Abbey in Mission, British Columbia, has a large baptismal pool at the entrance to their sanctuary. In it, a large boulder emerges from the pool of water and from it there gushes a continuous flow of water, symbolic of the rock in the wilderness. The soft, melodic sound of splashing water echoes throughout the nave, offering continual aural reminder of one's baptismal origin in the church. The sound of baptism is a companion to prayer, word, proclamation and meal.

Water

What is being done in your region to prevent contamination of water supplies by sewage or industrial wastes?

What help does your church or country provide to third world countries to aid well-digging, piping of water where it is needed, and prevention of disease transmission by means of water supplies?

Baptism is a water ritual, a cleansing bath, the experience of which is enhanced through the use of lots of water. Large, ample quantities of water are helpful in communicating the powerful biblical images of baptism. Small handfuls of water, fingers dipped from fingerbowl fonts to damp foreheads, wet carnations bounced off a baby's head, all conspire in their failure to communicate the deathly images of creation chaos, flood, exodus, burial with Christ. Baptism by immersion in a large baptismal pool perhaps best communicates these vivid images.

What's Happening Now?

How often do baptisms take place within your Sunday liturgy? Does this please you, or annoy you because it makes the service longer than usual?

Are there baptisms in your congregation at times other than the main Sunday service? Why is this and what do you think about this practice?

Is the liturgy of baptism planned and enacted in a way that builds up the whole congregation?

Is Easter a special time for baptisms in your congregation? Why or why not?

How are adults and parents of infants prepared for baptism in your congregation? Have you ever had the chance to participate in these preparation programs? Would you like to?

Can you see ways that you and your community could assist the newly baptized to continue their growth in the Christian faith?

Are The Connections Being Made?

How well do the non-verbal dimensions of the liturgy of baptism of your own Sunday liturgy express social justice values? Fail to express them? Contradict them?

Are There Changes To Be Made?

Identify aspects of the non-verbal part of the liturgy of baptism that you want to affirm, support and see continued. How will you support these?

Identify practices that need to be improved, corrected or changed. What alternatives to these practices can you envision? What can you do to bring about these changes?

In baptism we celebrate God's love, a love revealed in the life, death and resurrection of our Lord Jesus Christ, a love which has surrounded these children from the beginning.

In baptism we proclaim that God has acted to save these children. He washes them in his cleansing waters, and adopts them as members of his family, incorporating them into the living body of Christ.

In baptism we dedicate them to God's purposes knowing that even though we falter God will not, that he will continue through his Spirit the work begun this day, a work in which life triumphs over death.

Source Unknown

If You Have Energy For Just One Area, Start Here:

Ensure that ample amounts of water are used for baptism.
or
Initiate and/or take part in a process of preparation for adult candidates for baptism, or for parents who seek baptism for their children.

VERBAL DIMENSIONS

Both the core of the liturgy of baptism—the profession of faith and the baptism itself—and the prayers and actions that precede and follow these central elements need to be examined in order to see if they could be improved.

As those to be baptized, their parents—if the candidates are infants or children—sponsors, and ministers move to the font, a suitable hymn may be sung. This sets the mood, helps the assembly get into a baptismal frame of mind, encourages congregational participation, and accompanies the necessary movement.

Immediate Preparation for Baptism

The initial part of the liturgy of baptism may consist of declarations made by the candidates or their parents, by sponsors, and by the entire congregation; prayers for the candidates; brief instruction on the meaning of baptism; and a great prayer of thanksgiving over the water. In some churches there is also an explicit welcoming of the candidates, though in other churches this comes later in the liturgy.

Dialogue with the Minister

> *How does (or should) your civic community help single parents care for their children?*

> *What is being done to provide adequate and high quality day care for children in your community?*

Candidates are asked, directly or via parents or sponsors, if they freely seek baptism; there is to be no compulsion. In the case of the baptism of a child, parents and sponsors are also asked to declare an understanding and acceptance of their responsibilities to raise the children as Christians and to prepare them to affirm the baptismal commitment themselves at a suitable age. Part of such Christian raising of children is of course an attitude and actual training of discipleship.

Prayers and Instructions

> *Name a person whose commitment to Christian discipleship cost her/him personal freedom or death. Tell his or her story.*

> *What do you think should be done to budget adequately for social services, foreign aid, aid to farmers, etc., at the city, provincial/state and national levels?*

By means of both prayers and instructions the theology of baptism is explicated for the newly baptized as well as for the baptized assembly. Opportunity may be provided to involve the community, perhaps by preparing or leading the prayer; at least by remembering their own baptism. Such theological articulation in prayer and instruction also serves as a witness

Parental Responsibility

Will you be responsible for seeing that the child you present is nurtured in the faith and life of the Christian community?
   I will, with God's help.

Will you by your prayers and witness help this child to grow into the full stature of Christ?
   I will, with God's help.[10]

In Christian love you have presented these children for Holy Baptism. You should, therefore, faithfully care for them and help them in every way as God gives you opportunity, that they may bear witness to the faith we profess, and that, living in the covenant of their Baptism and in communion with the Church, they may lead godly lives until the day of Jesus Christ.

Do you promise to fulfil these obligations?
   I do.[11]

You have asked to have your children baptized. In doing so you are accepting the responsibility of training them in the practice of the faith. It will be your duty to bring them up to keep God's commandments as Christ taught us, by loving God and our neighbor. Do you clearly understand what you are undertaking?
   We do.[12]

90

Prayers for Those To Be Baptized

Let us now pray for these persons who are to receive the sacrament of new birth.

Deliver them, O Lord, from the way of sin and death.
  Lord, hear our prayer.

Open their hearts to your grace and truth.
  Lord, hear our prayer.

Fill them with your holy and life-giving Spirit.
  Lord, hear our prayer.

Teach them to love others in the power of the Spirit.
  Lord, hear our prayer.

Send them into the world in witness to your love.
  Lord, hear our prayer.

Bring them to the fullness of your peace and glory.
  Lord, hear our prayer.[13]

to those who may be more tentative or uncertain in their association with the baptized community. Finally, through prayer and instruction the costliness of discipleship is demonstrated, for it becomes clear that one's faith requires support and encouragement from God and from one another.

Prayer over the Water

What is being done to insure safe handling of industrial chemicals and safe disposal of nuclear and other wastes?

To what extent are you conscious of places around the world where people are seeking to escape from political, economic, or religious repression? How many such situations can you name and describe?

The water is graced and blessed with prayer. The theme of salvation through water is a prominent motif in the prayer over the baptismal water. Here is one example of such a blessing:

Holy God, mighty Lord, gracious Father:
We give you thanks, for in the beginning
your Spirit moved over the waters and you created
  heaven and earth.
By the gift of water you nourish and sustain us
  and all living things.
By the waters of the flood you condemned the
  wicked
and saved those whom you had chosen, Noah and
  his family.
You led Israel by the pillar of cloud and fire
  through the sea,
out of slavery into the freedom of the promised
  land.
In the waters of the Jordan your Son was baptized
  by John
and anointed with the Spirit.
By the baptism of his own death and resurrection
your beloved Son has set us free from the bondage
  to sin and death,
and has opened the way to the joy and freedom of
  everlasting life.
He made water a sign of the kingdom
and of cleansing and rebirth.
In obedience to his command, we make disciples of
  all nations,
baptizing them in the name of the Father,
and of the Son, and of the Holy Spirit.

Pour out your Holy Spirit, so that those who are
  here baptized
may be given new life.
Wash away the sin of all those who are cleansed
  by this water
and bring them forth as inheritors of your glorious
  kingdom.[14]

Prayer over the Water

*We thank you, Almighty God, for the gift of
water. Over water the Holy Spirit moved in
the beginning of creation. Through water you
led the children of Israel out of their bondage
in Egypt into the land of promise. In water
your Son Jesus received the baptism of John
and was anointed by the Holy Spirit as the
Messiah, the Christ, to lead us, through his
death and resurrection, from the bondage of
sin into everlasting life.*

*We thank you . . . for the water of bap-
tism. In it we are buried with Christ in his
death. By it we share in his resurrection.
Through it we are reborn by the Holy Spirit.
Therefore in joyful obedience to your Son, we
bring into his fellowship those who come to
him in faith, baptizing them in the name of
the Father, and of the Son, and of the Holy
Spirit.*

*Now sanctify this water by the power of
your Holy Spirit, that those who are here
cleansed from sin and born again, may continue for ever in the risen life of Jesus Christ
our Savior.*

*To him, to you, and to the Holy Spirit,
be all honour and glory, now and for ever.
Amen.*[15]

With such moving prayer, biblical imagery is remembered and brought to bear upon this baptism. Remembrance of God's saving activity of creation, in the flood, at the exodus, at Jesus' baptism, brings those ancient stories to life and incorporates them into the life of the faith community gathered to welcome a new member by baptism. Salvation history is washed into contemporary remembrance, enacted anew in this ritual bath.

There are strong social justice themes in those old stories. The Genesis creation account is a movement from chaos to order in which humanity is created in God's image. Humanity thus in a sense represents God within the created order and is charged with responsibilities to steward and care for creation. The flood is an instrument of God's wrath expressed at injustice, evil, corruption, and violence. The exodus, of course, is God's mighty action in hearing the lament of God's chosen people and in releasing those people from slavery and oppression in Egypt. In Jesus' baptism, Jesus stands in solidarity with the people in their expectation of a savior to free them. And in his baptism Jesus receives the spiritual anointing of affirmation from God's Spirit: *You are my beloved Son: with you I am well pleased.* Jesus is anointed royal heir and suffering servant. As the prayer reminds us, Jesus made water a sign not only of cleansing and rebirth, but also of the kingdom.

Profession of Faith and Baptism

In the profession of faith the candidates declare who the God is in whom they believe, to whom their lives now are totally dedicated, in whom they *live and move and have their being.* But the profession really has two movements, one "negative," the other "positive." In the former, candidates renounce, denounce, reject, spurn, turn away from, all that is not the one true God; furthermore, they promise to do so for the rest of their lives. Among the malignant influences and temptations upon which one's back must remain turned are the exploitation and enslavement of other men and women by whatever means, all forms of injustice, greed, abuse of relationships and so on. A personal and corporate ethic is defined by this renunciation.

The positive side of the profession is then expressed through a form of the ancient Apostles' Creed or, in some

The Baptismal Vows Reworded

Do you accept Jesus as your teacher, as the example whom you will always imitate and as the one in whom the mystery of God's love for the world has been fully revealed?

Do you dedicate yourself to seeking the kingdom of God and God's justice, to praying daily, to meditating on the gospels and to celebrating the Eucharist faithfully and devoutly?

Do you commit yourself to that spirit of poverty and detachment that Jesus enjoined on His disciples, and to resisting that spirit of consumerism and materialism that is so strong in our culture?

Do you accept your responsibility for building community, for being people of compassion and reconciliation, for being mindful of those who are poor and oppressed, and for truly forgiving those who have offended you?

Will you try to thank and praise God by your works and by your actions, in times of prosperity as well as in moments of suffering, giving loyal witness to the risen Jesus by your faith, by your hope and by the style of your living?

Do you surrender your lives to God as disciples and companions of Jesus? Do you believe that God is Lord of history, sovereign over nations and peoples, and that God's promise to redeem all of creation from its bondage to death and decay will one day be accomplished?

Do you believe in the Holy Spirit, the holy catholic Church, the communion of saints, the forgiveness of sins, and life everlasting?

W. E. Reiser[16]

Baptismal Renunciations

Do you renounce Satan and all the spiritual forces of wickedness that rebel against God?
I renounce them.

Do you renounce the evil powers of this world which corrupt and destroy the creatures of God?
I renounce them.

Do you renounce all sinful desires that draw you from the love of God?
I renounce them.[17]

Baptismal Affirmations

Will you continue in the apostles' teaching and fellowship, in the breaking of bread, and in the prayers?
I will, with God's help.

Will you persevere in resisting evil and, whenever you fall into sin, repent and return into the Lord?
I will, with God's help.

Will you proclaim by word and example the good news of God in Christ?
I will, with God's help.

Will you seek and serve Christ in all persons, loving your neighbor as yourself?
I will, with God's help.

Will you strive for justice and peace among all people, and respect the dignity of every human being?
I will, with God's help.[18]

churches, a modern creed. This confession of faith similarly articulates and defines both a personal and corporate ethic and faith stance.

Baptism in water then follows, whether by pouring or by immersion. This is accompanied and interpreted by the formula based on Matthew 29:19: *I baptize you in the name of the Father, and of the Son, and of the Holy Spirit.*

Some churches have the commendable practice of song at this point, allowing the community to joyfully greet each new sister and brother.

Welcoming the Newly Baptized

The people of God then proceed to welcome the new sisters and brothers in Christ Jesus, and in so doing they continue to draw out and express the meaning of baptism. In some churches this part of the liturgy of baptism is brief, in others quite extensive.

Laying On of Hands and Signing with the Cross

Often the newly baptized are signed on their foreheads with the cross to express that they now are Christ's, members of the church of Jesus Christ, entrusted with the ministry of Christ in today's world. This may be preceded or accompanied with the laying on of hands by the minister, a biblical gesture invoking the Holy Spirit and consecrating the person to ministry.

Oil or Chrism

Sometimes the signing with the cross is accompanied by anointing the heads of the newly baptized with oil or chrism (perfumed oil). Such an anointing bears with it rich biblical imagery of oil anointing royalty, priests, and those in need of healing. Such anointing with the sign of the cross on the brow makes tangible Christ's name as *the anointed One* and brings to life I Peter 2:9–10:

> But you are a chosen race, a royal priesthood,
> a holy nation, God's own people,
> that you may declare the wonderful deeds of him
> who called you out of darkness into his marvelous
>   light.
> Once you were no people but now you are God's
>   people.
> Once you had not received mercy but now you
>   have received mercy.

The anointing with oil is thus a mark of God's gift of grace and a commissioning to ministry in Christ's stead, empowered by the Holy Spirit, as one among the priestly people of God.

White Garment

What is being done to provide good schools, foster homes, sports programs, school lunches, etc., for children in your community?

How can your community concretely show concern for children in the third world?

In some communities, a white robe or garment is used to clothe the newly baptized. In the early church this practice was explained as a sign of forgiveness, of baptism's power of cleansing from sin, of putting on Christ. But it was also explained as a sign of a new and radiant life of holiness, the risen life of the Lord Jesus, the life by which the whole church now lives.

Lighted Candle

How are those with family difficulties helped and cared for in your community? separated or divorced? bereaved? dependent on drugs or alcohol?

What do you see as signs of hope in helping people start new lives?

Again in some churches, a lighted baptismal candle is presented to the newly baptized with these or similar words: *Let your light so shine before others that they may see your good works and glorify your Father in heaven.*[21] Other churches use the image of the watchful bridesmaids waiting for their Christ

Welcoming the Newly Baptized

Through Baptism God has made these new sisters and brothers members of the priesthood we all share in Christ Jesus, that we may proclaim the praise of God and bear his creative and redeeming Word to all the world.

We welcome you into the Lord's family. We receive you as fellow members of the body of Christ, children of the same heavenly Father, and workers with us in the kingdom of God.[19]

Let us welcome the newly baptized.

We receive you into the household of God. Confess the faith of Christ crucified, proclaim his resurrection, and share with us in his eternal priesthood.[20]

White Garment

(N., N.), you have become a new creation, and have clothed yourselves in Christ.

See in this white garment the outward sign of your Christian dignity. With your family and friends to help you by word and example, bring that dignity unstained into the everlasting life of heaven.[22]

Lighted Candle

*Receive the light of Christ,
to show that you have passed from darkness
  to light.*

*Let your light so shine before others
that they may see your good works
and glorify your Father in heaven.*[23]

here. Again, this symbolic presentation serves to link baptism to one's daily life in work, ministry and witness for Christ. The early church spoke of baptism as an *enlightenment;* the lighted candles may thus serve to sign the baptized person's movement from darkness to light.

After the Baptism

Baptism fittingly leads to eucharist. In thanksgiving, the holy meal among the holy people of God is a response to baptism and a sign of full initiation into the fellowship of the assembly. It is fitting therefore that the eucharist always be a part of the baptismal liturgy. The eucharist is, after all, the spiritual food that will nourish and sustain the spiritual life of these newly reborn sisters and brothers in Christ.

We are reminded of baptism through our daily and Sunday worship. Thus the making of the sign of the cross by the minister or worshipers is a baptismal reminder. So, too, is the practice of sprinkling water upon the assembly during the creed, or during the absolution of the penitential rite, or in place of the penitential rite. Simply having water in the font, accessible and available for people to see, touch and feel is a means of emphasizing baptism's role in the life of the community.

What's Happening Now?

In what ways do you personally welcome the newly baptized into the Christian community? Is the "welcoming" part of the liturgy of baptism meaningful and important to you? Through welcoming the newly baptized members of your own community, do you feel a sense of unity and solidarity with all baptized persons around the world?

Do you experience the baptism with water as the climax of the liturgy of baptism? How?

Do the laying on of hands, signing with the cross and anointing of oil communicate that the newly baptized are committed and empowered for ministry? How?

To what extent do the dialogue, prayers and instructions, and prayer over the water communicate to you that baptism has to do with ministry and social justice?

Are The Connections Being Made?

How well do the verbal dimensions of the liturgy of baptism of your own Sunday liturgy express social justice values? Fail to express them? Contradict them?

Are There Changes To Be Made?

Identify aspects of the verbal part of the liturgy of baptism that are good and that you want to affirm, support, and see continued. How will you support these?

Identify practices that need to be improved, corrected or changed. What alternatives to these practices can you envision? What can you do to bring about these changes?

If You Have Energy For Just One Area, Start Here:

Ensure that a great prayer of thanksgiving and blessing over water is used in your baptismal liturgy.
or
Evaluate and improve upon your practice—liturgical and social—of welcoming those newly baptized.

7. The Liturgy of the Eucharist

Introduction

The Eucharist and Social Justice

    The God We Worship
        Eucharist is thanksgiving to God
        The eucharist blesses the Creator and affirms and transforms creation
        The eucharist is an *anamnesis* or memorial of Christ
        The eucharist is an invocation of the Spirit

    The People Who Worship
        The eucharist is a meal for hungry people
        The eucharist is a meal of liberation
        The eucharist is a shared meal

    Our Mission and Ministry
        The eucharist leads to service of others
        The eucharist is a meal of the kingdom

The Liturgical Celebration

    Non-Verbal Dimensions
        The Day
        Architecture
        Hospitality
        Participation by all
        Sharing of ministry
        The bread and wine

    Verbal Dimensions
        Setting the table
        Prayer of thanksgiving
            Dialogue
            Preface

Holy, holy
Eucharistic prayer
Acclamations
The communion
Lord's Prayer
The peace
Breaking of bread and communion

In the liturgy of the eucharist the people of God, already fed by the word, now proceed to give thanks to God and to share the meal of the eucharistic bread and wine.

Many terms are used to describe this sacrament: *eucharist, the Lord's supper, the mass, holy communion, the table of the Lord, and divine liturgy* are among them. Each term emphasizes a particular nuance or perspective on the meal. Following an increasing ecumenical consensus, we usually will employ the term "eucharist," derived from a Greek word meaning "thanksgiving."

The liturgy of the eucharist has three main parts. In the first, the table is set and the food and other gifts brought up. The great prayer of thanksgiving, incorporating Jesus' words and actions at the last supper, follows. Finally, after the Lord's Prayer and (often) the sign of peace, holy communion is shared.

What Is Your Own Experience?

Think about your own experience of the liturgy of the eucharist. What meaning does it have for you?

Describe what actually happens as you and your community celebrate the eucharist.

The Eucharist and Social Justice

How might you describe the meaning of the celebration of the eucharist for yourself? What might you have to say about the relationship of the eucharist to social justice? How might the liturgy of the eucharist promote social justice values?

In fact, the wisdom and worship of the people of God through the centuries allow us to set out a clear vision of the relationship between the liturgy of the eucharist and social justice.

The eucharist is the sacramental meal of the baptized community. It is a meal instituted by Christ, continued at Christ's command and done in perpetual memory of Christ until his return. It is a meal of the Holy Spirit which anticipates the great feast to come in the kingdom of God. By means of this ritual meal, the assembly is united as we commune with Christ and with one another. Through the sacramental encounter with Christ, present in this meal of bread and wine, the baptized assembly is assured of forgiveness and the promise of life eternal. We are strengthened by this meal in faith and in ministry to faithfully *live between memory and hope.*

In sum, the eucharist declares who our God is, who we are, and what mission and ministry we are called to.

The God We Worship

Eucharist Is Thanksgiving to God

As Christ, at the last supper, instituted the eucharist with thanksgiving to God over bread and cup, so today the assembly of the baptized offers thanksgiving to God over bread and cup. The words of the eucharistic prayer may vary, but in the tradition and pattern of the Jewish *berekah* prayer, the presider voices the prayer of the assembly in offering thanksgiving to God for all God's saving acts: birthing creation, calling into being God's people, liberation, redemption and sanctification. But chiefly the church offers our prayer of praise and thanksgiving for the gift of Christ.

The Eucharist Blesses the Creator and Affirms and Transforms Creation

The eucharist testifies that God is not hostile to the creation, for elements of that creation, "stuff of the earth," bread and wine, are used to bear the presence of Christ into the assembly. Mere bread and wine are transformed. Similarly, the curse of human labor is transformed into a blessing, for the bread and wine bear with them signs of human labor. One can kaleidoscopically envision all that preceded that loaf—cultivating, sowing, reaping, threshing, grinding, mixing, kneading, baking—as it is borne to the altar in offering to God.

The Lord's Supper

But in the following instructions I do not commend you, because when you come together it is not for the better but for the worse. For, in the first place, when you assemble as a church, I hear that there are divisions among you; and I partly believe it, for there must be factions among you in order that those who are genuine among you may be recognised. When you meet together, it is not the Lord's supper that you eat. For in eating, each one goes ahead with his own meal, and one is hungry and another is drunk. What! Do you not have houses to eat and drink in? Or do you despise the church of God and humiliate those who have nothing? What shall I say to you? Shall I commend you in this? No, I will not.
1 Corinthians 11:17–22

Thanksgiving Litany

For the beauty and wonder of creation,
  We thank you. . . .

For all that is gracious in the lives of men
  and women, revealing the image of Christ,
  We thank you. . . .

For our daily food, for our homes and
  families and friends,
  We thank you. . . .

For minds to think and hearts to love,
  We thank you. . . .

For health, strength, and skill to work, and
  for leisure to rest and play,
  We thank you. . . .

For those who are brave and courageous,
  patient in suffering and faithful in
  adversity,
  We thank you. . . .

For all who pursue peace, justice, and truth,
  We thank you. . . .

[Today we give thanks especially for . . .]
  We thank you. . . .

For (. . . and) all the saints whose lives have
  reflected the light of Christ,
  We thank you. . . .[1]

General Thanksgiving Prayer

Accept, O Lord, our thanks and praise for all you have done for us. We thank you for the splendor of the whole creation, for the beauty of this world, for the wonder of life, and for the mystery of love. We thank you for the blessing of family and friends, and for the loving care which surrounds us on every side. We thank you for setting us tasks which demand our best efforts, and for leading us to accomplishments which satisfy and delight us. We thank you also for those disappointments and failures that lead us to acknowledge our dependence on you alone. Above all, we thank you for your Son Jesus Christ; for the truth of his word and the example of his life.[2]

Our gifts are similarly affirmed and transformed. We present these fruits of the earth, products of our labor to God. In turn, God presents them, transformed, back to us to free, sustain and nurture our lives of faith: the gifts of God for the people of God.

We, too, are affirmed and transformed. We common, ordinary people, creatures of God, are affirmed as the people of God and transformed as extraordinary: a royal priesthood, a holy nation, sent into the world in ministry.

The world may see mere bread and wine, but those with eyes to see bear witness to all of creation kneaded into this loaf and pressed into this wine.

The Eucharist Is an *Anamnesis* or Memorial of Christ

Jesus commanded his followers to do this thanksgiving meal in memory of him. In the eucharist, we remember all of Christ's saving actions—his incarnation and birth, ministry and teaching, his passion and death, resurrection and ascension, his promise and sending of the Holy Spirit—but we remember in such a way as to make contemporary and present that which is remembered. *Anamnesis* is thus not a resacrifice of Christ but a recollection that makes present the efficacy of Christ's redemption. It is a gathering of past actions of God into present proclamation and celebration. Further, the future is invoked, for the *anamnesis* looks forward as well to the fulfillment of God's reign when Christ shall return in glory. In the eucharistic memorial, past and future are wedded into the present moment as the assembly encounters the crucified and risen Lord in bread and wine.

In the eucharist we are thus called to participate in the paschal mystery even as we are sustained by it. We are invited to follow Christ, to take up our cross, lay down our lives. And where does this lead us? Jesus was often found among the poor, the oppressed, the ones excluded and trodden down by society. It is there that we will be called. While we encounter the crucified and risen Christ in the eucharist, chapter 25 of Matthew's gospel reminds us that in the world we will embrace Christ among the hungry, thirsty, naked, imprisoned, sick and unwelcomed.

The Eucharist Is an Invocation of the Spirit

The triune God is present in this meal. Through the *epiclesis* or invocation of the Holy Spirit, the eucharist prays for the enlivening, animating, empowering presence of the Holy Spirit upon the meal and upon the assembly. Baptism, Eucharist and Ministry declares: *The Church, as the community of the new covenant, confidently invokes the Spirit, in order that it may be sanctified and renewed, led into all justice, truth and unity, and empowered to fulfill its mission in the world.*

The People Who Worship

The Eucharist Is a Meal for Hungry People

We come to the Lord's table hungry and in need. To acknowledge that hunger and need is to admit that we are not gods, we are not self-sufficient and self-sustaining. Rather we are dependent upon God to feed us, to gift us with food from the creation and to gift us with himself as spiritual food. In the eucharist, within our worship, yet again idolatry is confronted as we confess our need of God.

The small bit of bread, the sip of wine feed us but leave us hungering, longing for more. Our need and dependence on God is maintained as we share a taste of the kingdom but continue to wait for its final consummation. Further, that sense of being still hungry binds us to a hungry world, awakens continually in us an awareness of *a world broken by unshared bread.*

The Eucharist Is a Meal of Liberation

Though scholars argue whether or not Jesus and his disciples were observing a passover meal that night before his death, imagery from the passover certainly is abundant within the eucharist: a meal bearing the presence of a remembered liberating action of God to sustain God's people into the future; eating the meal with girded loins, sandled feet and staff in hand—that is, ready for the journey of faith that proceeds from this feast; the image of Christ as the Lamb of God. In the passover the Jewish community recalls God liberating them from slavery and political tyrany. In the eucharist the baptized community remembers God liberating us from sin and death through Christ's redemption. The eucharistic meal of liberation is for a freed people, freed to serve God and humankind.

The Eucharist Is a Shared Meal

Not only are we dependent upon God, we are interdependent within the created order and within the baptized community. While our needs and expectations vary, our wounds and sorrows are diverse, we stand as equals around the Lord's table. Thus the eucharistic meal is communion not only with Christ but also with one another within the assembly of the baptized.

Such a celebration of communion and unity presumes a joyous and hopeful spirit of mutual forgiveness and reconciliation within the community of the church. Such reconciliation has implications for the whole world. Again, to quote Baptism, Eucharist, and Ministry, *The eucharistic celebration . . . is a constant challenge in the search for appropriate relationships in social, economic and political life. . . . All kinds of injustice, racism, separation and lack of freedom are radically challenged when we share in the body and blood of Christ.*

Pour out your Spirit upon the whole earth and make it your new creation. Gather your Church together from the ends of the earth into your kingdom, where peace and justice are revealed, that we, with all your people, of every language, race, and nation may share the banquet you have promised.[3]

Loving God, pour out your Holy Spirit upon us and upon these gifts, that they may be for us the body and bread of our Savior Jesus Christ. Grant that we may be for the world the body of Christ, redeemed through his blood, serving and reconciling all people to you.[4]

And that we might live no longer for
*   ourselves,*
but for him who died and rose for us,
he sent the Holy Spirit, his own first gift
for those who believe,
to complete his work in the world,
and to bring to fulfillment
the sanctification of all.[5]

When you have partaken
of this sacrament,
therefore,
or desire to partake of it,
you must in turn
share the misfortunes
of the fellowship . . .
all the unjust suffering
of the innocent,
with which the world
is everywhere filled to overflowing.
You must
fight, work, pray, and
—if you cannot do more—
have heartfelt sympathy

Martin Luther[6]

102

But when Jesus took bread and wine or a few fish and blessed God for them and shared them with his disciples, creation found its purpose once again. When the wood of the Cross, itself the innocent victim and unchoosing collaborator in man's inhumanity to man, became the means of expressing a hitherto undreamed of relationship between God and his people, the wood itself was redeemed. In each instance the true order of things was restored and justice reigned insofar as created things could now once again speak of God, the "lover of the human race." At the same time, and inseparably, they spoke of the right relationship that should exist between human beings. When Jesus took the bread, said the blessing, broke the bread and shared it, he demonstrated, unforgettably, the proper use of all material things. The early Christians realized this: they "eucharistized" their lives by blessing God in all things and by making their possessions available to one another. And when Jesus took the cup and gave thanks to God and passed it among his disciples, he rediscovered for the human race the joy of not claiming anything for one's own—not even life itself.

Mark Searle[7]

Anyone who celebrates the Lord's supper in a world of hunger and oppression does so in complete solidarity with the hopes and suffering of all men, because he believes that the Messiah invites all . . . to his table and because he hopes they will all sit at the table with him. In the mysteries, the feast separates the initiated from the rest of the world. But Christ's messianic feast makes its participants one with the physically and spiritually hungry all over the world.

Jurgen Moltmann[8]

In his life, Jesus often sat at table, sharing meals with the marginalized, scorned and ridiculed. Jesus welcomed them and was embraced by them. So the eucharistic meal is for all, inclusive and embracing of the outcast and forgotten, the lonely and lowly, the shy and the despised. All are welcome at this table of the Lord, for Christ is the host. In its equitable distribution, the eucharist constantly critiques our world and models a just means of sharing food among all.

The shared meal points not only to interdependence but also to the unity of the baptized. The one bread and one cup stand as visible signs of the unity within Christ's body, the church. There is one bread and one cup for all. There are not multiple loaves and cups—one for men, another for women, another for blacks, a fourth for homosexuals—but one bread and one cup calling us to, and demonstrating our unity in Christ.

Our Mission and Ministry

The Eucharist Leads to Service of Others

The life and ministry of Jesus, leading to his death and resurrection, were totally for others. At our eucharists we recall and repeat Jesus' words and actions at the last supper: *He took bread . . . and broke it and said, This is my body, which is for you. He took a cup . . . and said, This is my blood, shed for many for the forgiveness of sins.* Consider also three additional examples that demonstrate the connection between eucharist and servanthood.

In John's gospel, chapter 13, where one would expect to find the story of the institution of the eucharist, one reads instead the story of footwashing and Jesus setting his example of servanthood for the disciples. Jesus gives the new commandment to love one another as he loves them—giving his life for them. Implicit in its placement within the gospel, John links eucharist with service.

In Acts 2:44–46, Luke joins the worship of the breaking of bread with the equitable distribution of possessions and goods. Such linking of worship and sharing, Luke writes, provides that none be in any need. Such linking of worship and sharing in our time would provide the same care.

Finally, in 1 Corinthians 11, Paul exhorts the church to a social awareness and responsibility for the entire body of Christ when they gather for the eucharist. To participate in the eucharist without discerning the body within the assembly, Paul writes, is to eat and drink judgment. Such eating and drinking in our own time, unmindful of the entire baptized assembly, deserves the same severe critique. Yet again is raised the need to welcome all the baptized at the eucharistic feast.

The Eucharist Is a Meal of the Kingdom

The eucharist celebrates, anticipates, and participates in the reign of God. In its anticipation of the kingdom, the eucharistic meal is a foretaste of the great feast to come. The meal nourishes the baptized community to serve as "kingdom people," ministers already of the features of God's reign: mutual forgiveness, reconciliation and servanthood. This ministry is shared within the community and extended beyond the community in joyful, faithful witness to Jesus Christ. As Baptism, Eucharist, and Ministry states: *The eucharist . . . signifies what the world is to become: an offering and hymn of praise to the Creator, a universal communion in the body of Christ, a kingdom of justice, love and peace in the Holy Spirit.*

Reflect On This Vision

Our vision of the relationship between the liturgy of the eucharist and social justice may be summarized as follows:

The God We Worship
   Eucharist is thanksgiving to God
   The eucharist blesses the Creator and affirms
      and transforms creation
   The eucharist is an *anamnesis* or memorial of
      Christ
   The eucharist is an invocation of the Spirit
The People Who Worship
   The eucharist is a meal for hungry people
   The eucharist is a meal of liberation
   The eucharist is a shared meal
Our Mission and Ministry
   The eucharist leads to service of others
   The eucharist is a meal of the kingdom

In what respects does this vision agree with and affirm your own previous understanding of the relationship between Sunday worship and social justice?

What ideas regarding this relationship are new to you? How do you react to them?

An agonizing question presents itself to our minds. Why is it that in spite of hundreds of thousands of eucharistic celebrations, Christians continue as selfish as before? Why have the "Christian" peoples been the most cruel colonizers of human history? Why is the gap of income, wealth, knowledge and power growing in the world today—and that in favor of the "Christian" peoples? Why is it that persons and people who proclaim eucharistic love and sharing deprive the poor people of the world of food, capital, employment, and even land? Why do they prefer cigarettes and liquor to food and drink for the one-third of humanity that goes hungry to bed each night? Why are cards, cosmetics, pet dogs, horses and bombs preferred to human children? Why mass human sterilization in poor countries and affluence unto disease and pollution of nature among the rich?

Tissa Balasuriya[9]

Sacrifice is rather the gift of my life for the life of the world. Sacrifice in the model Jesus proposes means, "I spend myself so that others may live."

Mary Collins[10]

We give you thanks and praise, almighty God, for the gift of a world full of wonder, and for our life which comes from you. By your power you sustain the universe.[11]

Fountain of life and source of all goodness, you made all things and fill them with your blessing; you created them to rejoice in the splendor of your radiance.[12]

You formed us in your own image, giving the whole world into our care, so that, in obedience to you, our creator, we might rule and serve all your creatures.[13]

By Baptism we are all equally members of the Body. Where else in this world but in the Eucharist are king and beggar given the same gifts?

Louis Weil[14]

The Kingdom of God is like a seed planted
 in a woman's heart
  slowly, silently stretching it
  beyond family and friends, church and
    nation
  until one day that heart bursts open
  revealing a Table
  wider than the world
  warm as an intimate embrace.

To this Table everyone is invited
  no one is stranger, no one unfit;
  each brings a gift, work of one's own
  hands, heart, mind
  —a morsel for the Table—
  and there is always enough;
  enough because no one keeps hidden
  the bread of the morrow
  enough because in the sharing is
  the miracle of multiplication.

Around this Table everyone eats
  and no one is stuffed;
  each sips deeply of love unearned
  and offers the cup to another.

From this Table each rises
  strengthened by a morsel and a sip
  heart seeded
  pregnant.

Sister M. Robison[15]

The Liturgical Celebration

The vision of the church's best experience and wisdom regarding the liturgy of the eucharist almost certainly does not entirely coincide with our actual experience on Sunday morning.

We therefore need to ask: How can we change our actual practice so that vision and experience are in greater accord? How can we improve our Sunday liturgy? How can we make the community's great thanksgiving and holy meal as transforming as possible? In addition, we need to consider the individual elements of the liturgy of the eucharist in order to consider how they express and live out the vision of the relationship between the eucharist and social justice enunciated above.

NON-VERBAL DIMENSIONS

Most of the non-verbal dimensions of the liturgy of the eucharist will be mentioned only briefly, as they have been dealt with before. Nevertheless, they need to be examined to see if they may be improved.

The Day

What is being done to insure that workers have a day of rest and recreation? To what extent does Sunday shopping endanger this?

To what extent do Christian employers respect their Moslem and Jewish employees, whose days of religious observance are different than Sunday?

As for baptism, the Lord's day among the people of God is the proper setting for the eucharist. Each Sunday, which commemorates Christ's resurrection and anticipates the eighth day of the new creation, affords a regular occasion to celebrate the eucharist. Many churches are recovering the historic practice of celebrating the eucharist each week in a full liturgy of word and sacrament.

Architecture

As in earlier considerations, space and hospitality are critical in the eucharist. Does the worship space convey the sense of family gathered around the meal or are the people mere spectators? Is the table open, visible and accessible, or is it confined by railings or distanced against an east wall? Is there space for movement to encourage people to move about when engaged in the sharing of peace? Is there ample room for people to move easily from their seats to the table to share in the meal?

Hospitality

How does your community provide health care, adequate nutrition, and social services to the homebound?

What is being done to provide adequate facilities for the care of the elderly, mentally handicapped, and mentally ill?

Hospitality is critical for the presider and for the assembly. Does the presider incarnate a hospitable presence through gracious gesture and movement, presiding facing the assembly across the table? Or is the presider's presence alienating through mumbled prayer, sloppy vesture, or by presiding facing away from the people toward a wall? Do ministers of communion maintain eye and hand contact with the communicant, personalizing Jesus' declaration, *This is my body, my blood, given for you?* Or are they preoccupied with the physical task, fumbling with a cloth, distracted by others or conveying an assembly-line style of distribution?

The assembly practices hospitality in sharing. It is well to remember again that this meal is for all of the baptized, including the youngest and those who may be disabled. Some people may require assistance getting to and from the table; or indeed they may need to be served in their seats. The meal should not be rushed; time should be taken, graciously and hospitably, for all. In some congregations, children are included in a special way. Adults and children come row by row and form a circle around the altar/table. Only when the circle is complete do the ministers of communion begin to distribute bread and wine. This imagery of a complete circle of women, children and men emphasizes oneness and equality. The children who perhaps may not yet commune are recognized with a special blessing in remembrance of their baptism.

In some communities each communicant is named as they receive the bread and wine to intimately personalize the declaration, *for you.* While this is a hospitable and intimate affirmation of family in smaller worshiping communities, care must be exercised not to inadvertently exclude some whose names might not be known.

Increasingly in recent years, and following an ancient practice, the sick or those who are housebound and unable to participate in the community's eucharist in church are being

Consider now that sacramental act, the holy meal. This is the entire symbolic action in which the good news of our new life in the reign of God through our common baptismal death is proclaimed by rite, by gesture, by sign, by movement, by touch, by the honor and reverence given to all, by our eating and drinking commonly together. Just as the word is proclaimed and preached to all who will listen, without regard to station or status, so the baptismal death that accepts the new dominion and life of the reign of God, the kingdom, is offered to all on the sole condition of conversion. The banquet of the reign of God to which that baptismal death admits us is therefore no longer a domestic feast—not even one with an empty seat for the outsider and the reject. It is now an ecclesial feast, utterly common, free of distinction of sex, color, class, nation, property, power, even of family.

Robert W. Hovda[16]

Significantly, the word "companion" comes from Latin words that mean "with bread" . . . To break bread with another is to establish a bond, a companionship. This not only says what should be taking place in the eucharist itself, but also speaks to the point of establishing bonds of companionship, as a reflex action, through the sharing of bread with the whole [human] family.

Arthur Simon[17]

To share a meal in peace and harmony is a great grace, one of God's most precious gifts. We are a sacred and precious people, and that sacredness is not first celebrated in a large assembly. People need to see the gift that a meal carries, accept it with awareness and so enjoy at least some of their meals in an atmosphere of thanksgiving and reverence.

Begin with Sunday dinner or some other meal of the week which is important. . . . Or begin with meals at special times: holidays, birthdays, anniversaries.

Select a cup to set aside as the family's (or group's) "blessing cup". As it is used, it will become a sign of family solidarity and care for one another.

. . . begin the meal with a short reading from Scripture—a passage which speaks of the season or the occasion, or one which simply puts into words the hopes they share together. Those around the table might then offer petitions, express their joys or worries, or pray in silence for their needs.

Then fill the blessing cup with wine, or whatever beverage is enjoyed by all. Let the filling of the cup itself be a ceremonious act, which might be given to different . . . members at different times. The leader (a role which might

also be rotated) then recites a prayer of blessing and passes the cup around the table: "Blessed are you, (O Loving God) for all the gifts you have given to us. Blessed are you in Jesus, your son and our brother, who was poured out for us."

After the cup has been shared, the leader takes a piece of bread, breaks it, and passes it on a plate around the table, reciting another blessing: "Blessed are you, (O God, who is Mother and Father to us all) for giving us bread to eat. Blessed are you in Jesus, your son and our brother, who was broken for us. We recognize him and we give you thanks, here in the breaking of the bread."

After the bread is eaten, all might join hands around the table and recite the Lord's Prayer or sing a song. The meal continues as usual.

The Eucharist began around family tables with the simplest of prayers and gestures. The . . . table (of family/ friends) is still the best starting place for coming to understand what Christians mean by breaking the bread and sharing a cup in Jesus' name.

Tad Guzie[18]

---

remembered. Particular ministers of communion are deputed to go from the Sunday service to these brothers and sisters to share with them both the word that has been proclaimed for the community, and the bread and wine blessed and shared by the community.

Participation by All

Whom would you describe as discriminated against in your society? What is being done to overcome this?

It is particularly important to facilitate the participation of the whole assembly during the liturgy of the eucharist, as this part of the Sunday liturgy can easily become dominated by the presiding minister. In the first place, all listen closely in order to affirm the presider's prayer through their "Amen." In addition, there are in fact many occasions for corporate response: the preface dialogue, spoken or sung acclamations within and concluding the eucharistic prayer, sung doxologies to the prayer or hymns during the distribution of communion, periods of common silence for prayer and reflection during the sharing of the sacrament, and so on.

Sharing of Ministry

The eucharist is the meal of the baptized. It is fitting for members of the baptized community to share in the eucharistic ministries, for there are abundant opportunities: the care and preparation of the altar, including setting the table; the baking of bread or preparing of the wine; the presentation of the gifts; assisting the presiding minister in the distribution of bread and wine; providing choral or instrumental music during the distribution of communion; taking the eucharist to the sick, shut-in and imprisoned.

The Bread and Wine

What is being done to ensure that farmers and others who produce our food receive just incomes?

Should anything be done to limit advertising which promotes alcoholic consumption as part of a desirable lifestyle?

It is important that the bread and wine used for the eucharist be of such quality that they communicate their meaning through their size, shape, color, aroma and taste. Wafer bread, while convenient, fails to adequately communicate itself as real food. Some congregations use middle eastern pita bread. Such bread is commendable, and bears with it social justice associations in itself drawn from that troubled part of our world. Others use rich loaves symbolizing the bread of life that we all hunger for.

What's Happening Now?

Can you adequately see and hear what is done and said around the altar/table? Is ministry shared among ordained and lay ministers? Does the whole congregation really participate? Is there song? Is the bread and wine used real food? Are provisions made to take communion to the sick and others who cannot be present? Are all offered the cup?

Are The Connections Being Made?

How well do the non-verbal dimensions of the liturgy of the eucharist of your own Sunday liturgy express social justice values? Fail to express them? Contradict them?

Are There Changes To Be Made?

Identify aspects of the non-verbal part of the liturgy of the eucharist that are good and that you want to affirm, support and see continued. How will you support these?

Identify practices that need to be improved, corrected or changed. What alternatives to these practices can you envision? What can you do to bring about these changes?

If You Have Energy For Just One Area, Start Here:

Develop a ministry of taking communion to the sick, the homebound and the imprisoned directly following the celebration of the eucharist on Sunday.
or
Change the way communion is shared in your liturgy so that it is a more communal process and event.

VERBAL DIMENSIONS

The structured aspects of the liturgy of the eucharist may be divided into three parts. In the first of these the table is set and the gifts brought; the great prayer of thanksgiving provides the high point; and the concluding part of the liturgy is the holy communion.

All three parts of the eucharist need to be examined in order to see if they should be improved.

Setting the Table

What is being done to encourage young people to volunteer to serve the needy?

How are young people made aware of the needs of others in society?

In what some churches call the "offering" and others the "preparation of the gifts" or "preparation of the altar and the gifts," the bread and wine are presented at the altar and prepared. In some congregations, to emphasize communal participation in the eucharist, a family or group of people is invited to set the table. At the appropriate time these people gather at a point from which they can process to the altar. Each person carries a different article including a table cloth, the vessels for the bread and wine, the bread, wine and water, candles, flowers, and money offering. These are placed on—or, in the case of candles, flowers and collection baskets, near—the table, enabling the assembly to see the commonness and the holiness of the meal of bread and wine which they are about to share.

Prayer of Thanksgiving

The *eucharistic prayer*, or *great thanksgiving*, or by whatever name it is known, blesses God for creation and redemption past and present, and asks God's continued blessings on the people of God now and in the future.

Dialogue
The prayer begins with a dialogue between presider and assembly, which gathers and focuses our attention on the meal in our midst as we lift our hearts to God. Indeed, it is in the dialogue that the assembly authorizes and permits the presider to offer prayer on our behalf.

Preface
Then a preface is spoken or sung to set this particular eucharist into the context of the liturgical year. These prefaces are often rich with imagery of the paschal mystery, of the wider connection of this communion linking us to all of creation, to the church catholic, to the communion of saints. Consider for example, a preface for Easter, which concludes with this phrase:

Setting the Table. Churches vary in how this initial part of the liturgy of the eucharist is named. Among the terms used are *offertory, preparation of the gifts,* and *preparation of the gifts and the altar.*

Altar. Different churches tend to prefer the terms *altar, table* or *altar-table.* Here we use these interchangeably.

The Authors

. . . we offer with joy and thanksgiving what you have first given us—our selves, our time, and our possessions, signs of your gracious love. Receive them for the sake of him who offered himself for us, Jesus Christ our Lord.[19]

Blessed are you, Lord, God of all creation.
Through your goodness we have this bread to offer
which earth has given and human hands have made.
It will become for us the bread of life.
Blessed be God for ever.

Blessed are you, Lord, God of all creation.
Through your goodness we have this wine to offer,
fruit of the vine and work of human hands.
It will become our spiritual drink.
Blessed be God for ever.[20]

Prayer over the Gifts

God of heaven and earth,
receive our sacrifice of praise,
and strengthen us
for the perfect freedom of your service,
through our Savior Jesus Christ.[21]

The Lord be with you.
And also with you.

Lift up your hearts.
We lift them to the Lord.

Let us give thanks to the Lord our God.
It is right to give God thanks and praise.[22]

Preface. The relationship between *preface* and *eucharistic prayer* can be confusing. Strictly speaking, the *preface* is the first part of the total eucharistic prayer (and not simply an introduction to it). However, *eucharistic prayer* is used both for the whole prayer including the *preface,* and for the part of the total prayer that follows the *preface.*

The Authors

Holy, holy, holy Lord,
God of power and might,
heaven and earth are full of your glory.
Hosanna in the highest.

Blessed is he who comes in the name of the
  Lord.
Hosanna in the highest.[23]

And so, with Mary Magdalene and Peter and all the witnesses of the resurrection, with earth and sea and all their creatures, and with angels and archangels, cherubim and seraphim, we praise your name and join their unending hymn . . .

Holy, Holy

The preface concludes with a hymn of praise, the "Sanctus" or "Holy, Holy." This hymn images Isaiah's encounter with God's glorious majesty in the temple and Isaiah's attendant awe, awareness of sin, and readiness for mission (Isaiah 6:1–6). It further communicates Christ's triumphant entry into Jerusalem with the crowd's acknowledgement of Christ's paramount authority (Luke 19:27–46). We sing "Hosanna," which means "Save us." In our song we remember the imagery of Luke that if the multitude were silent the very stones would cry out. All of creation joins us in offering thanks and praise to our Creator and Redeemer.

Eucharistic Prayer

What do you see as signs of hope in the liberation of people from repressive situations in your community and around the world?

Around the year 150, Justin Martyr described the liturgical president praying "as well as he is able" over the eucharist. The use of a full eucharistic prayer of thanksgiving is increasingly common and to be commended. It is in keeping with the Jewish practice—Jesus' practice—of thanksgiving prayer which Christ commanded the night before his death.

Such a prayer of thanksgiving first remembers and praises God for creation, and then for all God's saving actions through history: flood, call of Israel, exodus, the ministry of the prophets, and so on—and most especially and completely, the life, ministry, death and resurrection of Jesus Christ.

A second element is *epiclesis,* the invocation of the presence and transforming action of the Holy Spirit upon the bread and wine and upon the assembly.

Following the recital of the central words and actions of Jesus at the last supper, we proclaim that what we are doing today is our *anamnesis* or memorial of God's saving work in Christ.

Further prayers follow. Often these are for the unity of the church and that the church may carry out the ministry entrusted to us by Christ. There is also a looking forward to the final fulfillment of God's reign. One such prayer reads:

Gather your church together from the ends of the earth into your kingdom, where peace and justice are revealed, that we, with all your people, of every language, race, and nation, may share the banquet you have promised.

In some traditions, the eucharistic prayer included *dyptichs,* specific prayers of intercession for particular causes. These prayers voiced precise need and lament at the very point where the assembly prepared to share the "bread for the morrow" in the kingdom meal.

Finally, the great prayer of thanksgiving concludes with a profound but exultant doxology or song of praise.

Acclamations

The eucharistic prayer includes the assembly's participation in the memorial acclamation, *Christ has died. Christ has risen. Christ will come again.* Such acclamation articulates themes of justice, redemption and hope, and in some churches may be joined to the *maranatha, Come, Lord Jesus,* and again with *Come, Holy Spirit.* The eucharistic prayer ends with the assembly's acclamation of affirmation: *Amen, Amen, Amen.*

The Communion

Lord's Prayer

Immediately following the eucharistic prayer, and in preparation for the communion, the assembly, all together, prays the Lord's Prayer. It is as if to say that all our prayers of praise and thanksgiving, intercession and lament, joy and sorrow have been prayed. Now we gather and sum them up in the prayer that Jesus taught us to pray. It is altogether fitting that the Lord's Prayer is prayed just at this point before the breaking and sharing, for this prayer also gathers remembrance and anticipation into the present moment and reminds us that Christ is our only intercessor. The Lord's Prayer does this with potent thematics of social justice, for it is a prayer that explicitly beseeches God's reign now.

The prayer is addressed to almighty God with the intimacy of a parental endearment. The plural address, "our," reminds us that we are a community. The hallowing of God's name and beseeching the kingdom is a plea on behalf of all creation that all might know God's name, that God's reign may come in all its fullness. To pray for daily bread is to beg for more than our daily ration of food. The phrase may also be translated "our bread for the morrow," thereby asking God for food from the kingdom meal for today. With that understanding in mind the Lord's Prayer is even more intimately connected to the eucharist.

The remaining petitions pray that the kingdom be realized now in our ethical lifestyles. We pray that we may already

Let us proclaim the mystery of faith.

Christ has died.
Christ is risen.
Christ will come again.

Dying you destroyed our death,
rising you restored our life.
Lord Jesus, come in glory.[24]

A few references that explore the eschatological character of the Lord's Prayer:

The Prayers of Jesus, by Joachim Jeremias (Philadelphia: Fortress Press 1978)

"The Pater Noster," in *New Testament Essays,* by Raymond E. Brown (Garden City: Image Books 1968)

"Your Kingdom Come: Notes for Bible Study," in *Your Kingdom Come: Mission Perspectives* (Geneva: World Council of Churches 1980)

112

The Lord's Prayer: A Paraphrase

O God far above and beyond our grasp, yet close to us like a parent:

Let the time come soon when you are recognized by all as God.

That is, when you establish your supreme and good and just rule over your whole creation.

Yes, let the time come soon when your gracious plan for salvation becomes a reality on earth, as it now is in heaven.

While we wait for that day, let us already now enjoy the foretaste of the messianic banquet as we share in the bread that sustains our bodies.

In order to make us worthy of that community, forgive us what we have done wrong to our brothers and sisters as we have already forgiven those who did wrong to us; for we know that we are and must be the mutually forgiven community, your community of these end times.

And see to it that we are not tested beyond our strength, for we know that Satan can destroy us—unless you rescue us out of his ferocious grip.

Krister Stendahl[25]

Sign of Peace. This liturgical action is variously called the *sign of peace, greeting of peace,* or simply *the peace.*

The Authors

practice mutual forgiveness, that we not be tested beyond our capacity. It concludes with a doxology of praise.

To thus pray the Lord's Prayer is to dare to pray in the name of Jesus to God with childlike trust. It is to ask God to reveal his glory and to grant already today the bread of life. It is to beseech God's forgiveness, even as a pledge to practice forgiveness is offered. In the midst of constant testing and threats of apostasy, the Lord's Prayer begs now for the reign of God over the life of God's children.

The Peace

What do you think should be done to control the arms race?

How would you like to redirect funds now used on military spending?

At the conclusion of the Lord's Prayer is an appropriate place to share a sign of reconciliation and peace though we have already seen that it is equally appropriate following the proclamation and preaching of the word.

Ample time and space should be provided for the sharing of the peace by the community. This is not chit-chat, small-talk, social time. This is the mark of a forgiven people offering mutual peace and reconciliation: affirmation and communication of the peace that is ours in Christ. The peace may be shared verbally (for example, *Peace, The peace of Christ, The peace of Christ be with you*), in combination with handshake, embrace, or kiss.

Breaking of Bread and Communion

How do you express solidarity with the hungry in your own community and throughout the world?

What is being done to share food and other resources with those less fortunate than yourselves?

Jesus broke bread and gave it. So do we in memory of him. Both bread and cup are prayed over. Both bread and cup are to be shared among all.

The use of a loaf of real bread—leavened or unleavened—is to be commended over the use of individual wafers. The breaking or sharing of one loaf more adequately bears the image of unity and wholeness in the body of Christ. An early prayer from around the year 100 presents the bread as a sign of unity as well as of God's reign:

As this broken bread was scattered over the mountains and when brought together became one, so let your church be brought together from the ends of the earth into your kingdom.

Bread, broken and shared, is a sign of the longing for unity within the community and within the church catholic.

In similar fashion, one cup of wine more adequately conveys the oneness of the church. Individual wine glasses serve to heighten a sense of disunity and individualism which is best avoided. The serving of wine only to the clergy and assisting ministers, or for example only to the bridal party at a wedding, similarly serves to fragment the sense of community that should prevail within worship.

The oneness and unity symbolized in the bread and cup offers a vision of the unity of the church, the unity for which Jesus prayed the night he instituted the eucharist. It thus critiques our fragmented, denominationalized churches, calls us to ecumenical awareness and cooperation.

What's Happening Now?

Do you experience the liturgy of the eucharist as a real, though special meal? As a meal of liberation?

Does the hunger you feel for the food of the eucharist remind you of the many people around the world who are materially hungry? How?

Does the sharing of the eucharistic meal of liberation lead you, and lead your community, to concrete actions in solidarity with those who experience oppression?

At the Breaking of the Bread

"I am the bread of life," says the Lord. "Whoever comes to me will never be hungry; whoever believes in me will never thirst."

Taste and see that the Lord is good; happy are they who trust in him.

We break this bread to share in the body of Christ.

We, being many, are one body, for we all share in the one bread.

Creator of all, you gave us golden fields of wheat, whose many grains we have gathered and made into this one bread.

So may your Church be gathered from the ends of the earth into your kingdom.

"I am the bread which has come down from heaven," says the Lord.

Give us this bread for ever.

"I am the vine, you are the branches."

God of promise, you prepare a banquet for us in your kingdom.

Happy are those who are called to the supper of the Lamb.[26]

The gifts of God for the people of God. Thanks be to God.[27]

The body of Christ (given for you). The blood of Christ (shed for you).[28]

The body of Christ, the bread of heaven. The blood of Christ, the cup of salvation.[29]

114

I believe in people, as I believe in God
I believe in the sons and the daughters of
   humankind
I believe we are the image of the Divine
I have faith in my brothers and sisters
I have confidence in us, the people of God
I am the keeper of my tribe
I am the protector of life
I am the song of my ancestors
I am my grandchildren's hymn
I am the suffering cry
I am the shout of an angry race

We are our own salvation
We are our own strength
We are God within us
Erupting deliverance

      Declaration of Faith and Commitment,
           Tribal Filipino Sunday[30]

When you greet others during the sign of peace, what feelings do you experience? What meaning does this action have for your worshiping community?

Are The Connections Being Made?

How well do the verbal dimensions of the liturgy of the eucharist of your own Sunday liturgy express social justice values? Fail to express them? Contradict them?

Are There Changes To Be Made?

Identify aspects of the verbal part of the liturgy of the eucharist that are good and that you want to affirm, support and see continued. How will you support these?

Identify practices that need to be improved, corrected or changed. What alternatives to these practices can you envision? What can you do to bring about these changes?

If You Have Energy For Just One Area, Start Here:

Ensure that the bread used for communion is really bread, and that the cup is shared by all.
or
Make the sign of peace a regular part of your Sunday liturgy, or take steps to improve the quality of the interaction that it involves.

8. The Sending Forth of God's People

Introduction

Sending Forth and Social Justice

The Liturgical Celebration

[We] need to experience a sense of rhythm between our 'gathering' to celebrate the death and resurrection of Christ in Holy Communion, and our 'dispersal' to continue the eucharistic celebration elsewhere—in our daily vocations, personal relationships, use of material blessings, caring and learning about people who suffer unjustly, and efforts to alter the value society puts on them so that their suffering will not dehumanize us all.

Arthur Simon[1]

Does the conclusion of your Sunday liturgy—which we are calling "the sending forth of God's people" or "the liturgy of sending forth"—have any meaning and significance aside from the purely practical one of allowing everyone to go home? And if there is some deeper purpose, then how, if at all, is it relevant to social justice? How might it promote social justice values?

In fact, the wisdom of the Christian tradition tells us that the liturgy of sending forth has a very profound meaning and that there is a clear and intrinsic relationship between this part of our Sunday liturgy and social justice.

As with the liturgy of gathering, the concluding part of our Sunday liturgy is quite simple: we just go forth.

Again, most of the liturgy of sending forth is non-verbal, informal and somewhat spontaneous; the community's worship continues long after the presiding minister steps down and the printed service of the bulletin or worship-book concludes.

There is of course a formal, structured and more verbal phase of the liturgy of sending forth, and this tends to vary considerably from church to church. Generally, however, it includes at least prayer, benediction, commissioning, dismissal and song, and probably announcements.

What Is Your Own Experience?

Think about your own experience of the liturgy of sending forth. What meaning does it have for you?

Describe what actually happens as you and your community are sent forth.

. . . At each Sunday liturgy, the congregation prays together the Missioning Prayer:

Your eucharist, Lord Jesus, is a memorial of
• your life given for us
• your body broken for us
• your love poured out for us.
May our thanksgiving for your
unbelievable gift
be so genuine that we too,
may become
bread broken and shared
for each other.

People at St. Joseph's "mission" reach out at each liturgy—to bring communion to those parishioners who might not have been able to be physically present; to be good news for each other; to be the leaven in the bread "that we may become bread broken and shared for each other. "Eucharist is central. Once again, the bread becomes so much more than a sign. It is central to the community, and it is always broken and shared.

Delia Carley, pastoral team
St. Joseph's Parish, Ottawa, Ontario[2]

Sending Forth and Social Justice

The liturgy draws to a conclusion. Having worshiped God with our fellow members of the community, we now prepare to scatter, going our separate ways. We go back to the rest of the Lord's day, to spend it in an appropriate manner. We go back to our regular lives of family life, work and social interaction. We go back to do Christ's work in all aspects of our lives, to be disciples and believers wherever we are.

But does our worship really end? We return to the world transformed. We have been strengthened, challenged, empowered with new vision, encouraged with new hope and joy. Our worship thus continues as it is transformed into service, ministry, prayer, acts of mercy and justice until next the assembly of the baptized gathers. It is this dimension of worship to which the Orthodox refer when they speak of *the liturgy beyond the Liturgy.*

The commission to ministry contained in the sending-forth rite propels us in service into all the world. We are sent as servants of Christ, ministering to all in any need: the sick, hungry, the abandoned and abused, those who are lost and lonely, those who are oppressed and imprisoned, the grieving, and those who have lost hope. The categories of ministry go on and on. The people encountered and the ministries performed are numberless.

. . . we can no longer celebrate the Eucharist with eyes closed to the needs of others. The Eucharist commits the individual and the Christian community to the transformation of the world.

. . . we have something to learn from the Orthodox Church which talks about "the liturgy after the Liturgy." By this they mean that worship at the holy table of the Lord must flow into an active service on the 'second altar' of freeing our needy sisters and brothers.

Dermot Lane[3]

118

A Commitment Ceremony From Asia

VOICE 1: We seek to change our lives and to change the organization of society.

VOICE 2: In order to help build a new society and a new humanity, a new heaven and a new earth.

VOICE 1: We seek a transformation of mind and spirit, a total reshaping of the structures of society, a revolution in human relationships.

VOICE 2: We seek a new pattern of relationships between leaders and people, administrators and workers, teachers and pupils, parents and children, priests and laity, women and men.

VOICE 1: We seek sharing of power and resources of leadership and responsibility.

VOICE 2: We seek a new order of love, justice and peace that all may care.

VOICE 1: We seek liberation for all those who are oppressed.

VOICE 2: We seek to commit ourselves to the struggle for all to be free.

ALL: We commit ourselves to translate principle into practice as far as we can day by day, alongside the people, according to Your will.

Christian Conference of Asia[4]

In a very real sense, this sending forth to ministry is an embodiment of our prayers and intercessions. God uses the people of God to effect God's saving, healing, reconciling presence in the world. We become instruments of Christ's peace and grace in our ministry.

A congregation in Michigan has a stained glass window over the entrance doors to the nave. From inside the sanctuary, with the glass illumined, one observes that the window depicts a map of their city and community. Beneath the window is a sign. It is the last thing read before the worshipers leave the building and return to the world. It reads: "Servants' Entrance."

Reflect On This Vision

In what respects does our vision of sending forth agree with and affirm your own previous understanding of the relationship between Sunday worship and social justice?

What ideas regarding this relationship are new to you? How do you react to them?

The Liturgical Celebration

As with gathering, in leaving there is a formal and planned component and an informal and spontaneous dimension. Both need to be examined to see if they can be improved.

The formal phase is quite brief. It may consist of a hymn, prayer, scripture text, benediction, dismissal, or some combination of these. In addition, parish announcements might precede the final dismissal to ministry. These announcements are brief, concise and bear on opportunities and needs for ministry, witness and mission, rather than chronicling a long list of meeting dates.

In concluding, a strong and challenging, yet comforting and reassuring statement of benediction often will be made. Perhaps it uses the ancient words of Aaron, or more contemporary phrases, but the intent is to bless the assembly once more in the name of the triune God, and then commission us in ministry: "Go in peace; serve the Lord."

A concluding hymn may be sung in response to our encounter with Christ in word and sacrament. Some churches use Luke's song of Simeon, the *Nunc Dimittis*, where with the aged seer in the temple the assembly sings that God would let them depart in peace for they have seen with their own eyes God's salvation. The intent is to conclude, send forth, and assure the assembly that God goes with us.

The words may be followed by an organ or instrumental postlude or by silence. The rite is simple, clear and straightforward, unencumbered by elaborate ceremonies of extinguishing candles or maudlin sounding of chimes.

The informal, spontaneous phase is the physical leave-taking of the community. Hospitality plays a role here as well, assisting people with their coats, acknowledging one another's presence and yet again affirming a sense of *koinonia* or communion.

One's leave-taking need not be hasty. For this is a prime occasion for fellowship—the mutual conversion and consolation of the community. The provision of refreshments may enhance this time of social, community interaction.

Prayer after Communion

O God,
may we who have shared in holy things
never fail to serve you in your world,
and so come to the fullness of joy,
in the name of Jesus Christ our Lord.[5]

Prayer after Communion

Eternal God,
comfort of the afflicted and healer of the
*   broken,*
you have fed us this day at the table of life
*   and hope.*
Teach us the ways of gentleness and peace,
that all the world may acknowledge
the kingdom of your Son Jesus Christ our
*   Lord.*[6]

What's Happening Now?

To what extent do you experience the conclusion of your Sunday liturgy as the end of something, or the beginning of something, or both? Are you relieved to "have it over with," or challenged to carry something from worship into the rest of Sunday and through the week?

Describe the way your Sunday liturgy really and effectively com-

120

Benedictions

The Lord bless you and keep you.
The Lord make his face shine on you and be
gracious to you.
The Lord look upon you with favor and give
you peace. Amen.[7]

The [God] of mercies has given us
an example of unselfish love
in the sufferings of his only Son.
Through your service of God and neighbor
may you receive his countless blessings.
Amen.

You believe that by his dying
Christ destroyed death for ever.
May he give you everlasting life. Amen.

He humbled himself for our sakes.
May you follow his example
and share in his resurrection. Amen.

May almighty God bless you,
the Father, and the Son, and the Holy Spirit.
Amen.[8]

missions individuals and the community to ministry (or fails to do so).

Are The Connections Being Made?

How well does the way the sending forth of God's people is celebrated in your own Sunday liturgy express social justice values? Fail to express them? Contradict them?

Are There Changes To Be Made?

Identify practices of sending forth that are good and that you want to affirm, support and see continued. How will you support these?

Identify practices that need to be improved, corrected or changed. What alternatives to these practices can you envision? What can you do to bring about these changes?

If You Have Energy For Just One Area, Start Here.

Ensure that the sending forth contains a strong element of commissioning for ministry.
or
Make sure that hospitality is exercised well at the end of your Sunday liturgy.

Bibliography

A. Books

Apostolos-Cappadona, Diane (ed.). *The Sacred Play of Children*. New York: The Seabury Press, 1983.

Avila, Rafael. *Worship and Politics*. Maryknoll: Orbis Books, 1981.

Balado, J. L. G. *The Story of Taize*. London and Oxford: Mowbray and Co. Ltd., 1981.

Balasuriya, Tissa. *The Eucharist and Human Liberation*. Maryknoll: Orbis Books, 1979.

Baptism, Eucharist and Ministry. Geneva: World Council of Churches, 1982.

Bell, Bernard. *The Altar and the World: Social Implications of the Liturgy*. London: Dobson, 1946.

Bernier, Paul. *Bread Broken and Shared: Broadening Our Vision of Eucharist*. Notre Dame: Ave Maria Press, 1981.

Bishops' Committee on Liturgy. *Environment and Art in Catholic Worship*. Washington, D.C.: U. S. Catholic Conference, 1978.

Brown, Robert McAfee. *Unexpected News: Reading the Bible With Third World Eyes*. Philadelphia: The Westminster Press, 1984.

Brueggemann, Walter; Parks, Sharon; and Groome, Thomas H. *To Act Justly, Love Tenderly, Walk Humbly: An Agenda for Ministers*. New York: Paulist Press, 1986.

Caemmerer Jr., Richard R. *Visual Art in the Life of the Church*. Minneapolis: Augsburg Publishing House, 1983.

Camara, Dom Helder. *The Desert Is Fertile*. Maryknoll: Orbis Books, 1974.

Cardenal, Ernesto. *The Gospel in Solentiname*. (4 volumes) Maryknoll: Orbis Books, 1978.

Chafe, Joanne M. (ed.). *Adult Faith, Adult Church*. Ottawa: Canadian Catholic Conference of Bishops, 1986.

Challenge to the Church: A Theological Comment on the Political Crisis in South Africa ("The Kairos Document"). Braamfontein, South Africa: The Kairos Theologians, 1985.

Cochrane, Arthur. *Eating and Drinking With Jesus: An Ethical and Biblical Inquiry*. Philadelphia: The Westminster Press, 1974.

Debuyst, Frederic. *Modern Architecture and Christian Celebration*. London: Lutterworth Press, 1968.

Deiss, Lucien. *Early Sources of the Liturgy*. Collegeville: The Liturgical Press, 1975.

———. *It's the Lord's Supper: Eucharist of Christians*. New York: Paulist Press, 1976.

Dix, Dom Gregory. *The Shape of the Liturgy*. London: Dacre Press, 1975.

Eaton, John. *Vision in Worship: The Relation of Prophecy and Liturgy in the Old Testament*. London: SPCK, 1981.

Egan, John P. *Baptism of Resistance, Blood and Celebration*. Mystic, Conn.: Twenty-Third Publications, 1983.

Egge, Mandus A. *Worship: Good News in Action*. Minneapolis: Augsburg Publishing House, 1973.

Elliott, Charles. *Praying the Kingdom: Towards a Political Spirituality*. London: Darton, Longman and Todd, 1985.

Environment and Art in Catholic Worship. Washington, D.C.: National Conference of Catholic Bishops, 1978.

Field, Anne. *From Darkness to Light: What It Meant to Become a Christian in the Early Church*. Ann Arbor: Servant Books, 1978.

Fjedur. *Freedom Is Coming: Songs of Protest and Praise from South Africa*. Uppsala: Utryck, 1984.

For All God's People: Ecumenical Prayer Cycle. Geneva: World Council of Churches, 1983.

Fourez, Gerard. *Sacraments and Passages: Celebrating the Tensions of Modern Life*. Notre Dame: Ave Maria Press, 1983.

Freire, Paulo. *Pedagogy of the Oppressed*. New York: Herder and Herder, 1971.

Gjerding, Iben and Kinnamon, Katherine (eds.). *No Longer Strangers: A Resource for Women and Worship*. Geneva: WCC Publications, 1983.

Gonzalez, Justo L. and Gonzalez, Catherine G. *Liberation Preaching: The Pulpit and the Oppressed*. Nashville: Abingdon Press, 1980.

Grassi, Joseph A. *Broken Bread and Broken Bodies: The Lord's Supper and World Hunger*. Maryknoll: Orbis Books, 1985.

Groome, Thomas H. *Christian Religious Education: Sharing Our Story and Vision*. New York: Harper and Row, 1980.

Guardini, Romano. *Sacred Signs*. Dublin: Veritas Publications, 1979.

Gutierrez, Gustavo. *A Theology of Liberation*. Maryknoll: Orbis Books, 1973.

———. *We Drink From Our Own Wells*. Maryknoll: Orbis Books, 1984.

Häring, Bernard. *The Eucharist and Our Everyday Life*. New York: The Seabury Press, 1979.

Hellwig, Monika K. *The Eucharist and the Hunger of the World*. New York: Paulist Press, 1976.

Heschel, Abraham J. *The Prophets*. New York: Harper and Row, 1962.

Hessel, Dieter T. (ed.) *Social Themes of the Christian Year*. Philadelphia: The Geneva Press, 1983.

Holland, Joe and Henriot, Peter. *Social Analysis: Linking Faith and Justice*. Maryknoll: Orbis Books in collaboration with Washington, D.C.: The Center of Concern, 1983.

Hovda, Robert. *Dry Bones: Living Worship Guides to Good Liturgy*. Washington, D.C.: The Liturgical Conference, 1973.

———. *Strong, Loving and Wise: Presiding in Liturgy*. Washington, D.C.: The Liturgical Conference, 1976.

Huck, Gabe. *Liturgy With Style and Grace: A Basic Manual for Planners and Ministers.* Chicago: Liturgy Training Program, 1978.

Jacobson, J. Robert. *Besides Women and Children: A Handbook for Parents and Pastors on Infant and Child Communion.* Calgary: Foothills Lutheran Press, 1979.

Jeremias, J. *The Prayers of Jesus.* Philadelphia: Fortress Press, 1978.

Jones, Cheslyn; Wainwright, Geoffrey; Yarnold, Edward. (eds.) *The Study of Liturgy.* New York: Oxford University Press, 1978.

Kameeta, Zephania. *Why, O Lord? Psalms and Sermons from Namibia.* Philadelphia: Fortress Press, 1986.

Kavanagh, Aidan. *Elements of Rite: A Handbook of Liturgical Style.* New York: Pueblo Publishing Company, 1982.

Koenig, John. *New Testament Hospitality: Partnership With Strangers as Promise and Mission.* Philadelphia: Fortress Press, 1985.

Lathrop, Gordon and Ramshaw-Schmidt, Gail (eds.). *Lectionary for the Christian People-A.* New York: Pueblo Publishing Company, 1986.

A Lutheran Agenda for Worship. Geneva: Department of Studies, Lutheran World Federation, 1979.

Lutheran Book of Worship. Minneapolis: Augsburg Publishing House, 1978.

Maldonado, Luis and Power, David (eds.). *Symbol and Art in Worship.* New York: The Seabury Press, 1980.

Marx, Paul B. *Virgil Michel and the Liturgical Movement.* Collegeville: The Liturgical Press, 1957.

Maxwell, John. *Worship in Action: A Parish Model of Creative Liturgy and Social Concern.* Mystic, Conn.: Twenty-Third Publications, 1981.

Meehan, Francis X. *A Contemporary Social Spirituality.* Maryknoll: Orbis Books, 1982.

Micks, Marianne H. *The Future Present: The Phenomenon of Christian Worship.* New York: The Seabury Press, 1970.

Morland, David. *The Eucharist and Justice: Do This in Memory of Me.* London: Commission for International Justice and Peace of England and Wales, 1980.

Muller-Fahrenholz, Geiko. . . . *And Do Not Hinder Them: An Ecumenical Plea for the Admission of Children to the Eucharist.* Geneva: World Council of Churches, 1982.

The Murphy Center for Liturgical Research. *Made, Not Born: New Perspectives on Christian Initiation and the Catechumenate.* Notre Dame: University of Notre Dame Press, 1976.

Neville, Gwen Kennedy and Westerhoff III, John. *Learning Through Liturgy.* New York: Seabury Press, 1978.

Newman, David. *As Often As You Do This . . . : Toward More Frequent Celebration of the Lord's Supper in The United Church of Canada.* Toronto: The United Church of Canada, 1981.

Parvey, Constance (ed.). *The Community of Women and Men in the Church: The Sheffield Report.* Geneva: World Council of Churches, 1983.

Polish, Daniel F. and Fisher, Eugene J. (eds.). *Liturgical Foundations of Social Policy in the Catholic and Jewish Traditions.* Notre Dame: University of Notre Dame Press, 1983.

Power, David N. *Unsearchable Riches: The Symbolic Nature of Liturgy.* New York: Pueblo Publishing Company, 1984.

Ramshaw, Elaine. *Ritual and Pastoral Care.* Philadelphia: Fortress Press, 1987.

Ramshaw-Schmidt, Gail. *Christ in Sacred Speech: The Meaning of Liturgical Language.* Philadelphia: Fortress Press, 1986.

———. *God's Food: The Relationship Between Holy Communion and World Hunger.* Philadelphia: Division for Parish Services, Lutheran Church in America, 1984.

———. *Letters for God's Name.* New York: The Seabury Press, 1984.

Report on the World Conference on Mission and Evangelism. *Your Kingdom Come: Mission Perspectives.* Geneva: World Council of Churches, 1980.

Rite of Christian Initiation of Adults. Ottawa: Canadian Conference of Catholic Bishops, 1988.

Rordorf, Willy (et al.). *The Eucharist of the Early Christians.* New York: Pueblo Publishing Company, 1978.

Ruether, Rosemary Radford. *Sexism and God-Talk: Toward a Feminist Theology.* Boston: Beacon Press, 1983.

Schaull, Richard. *Heralds of a New Reformation: The Poor of South and North America.* Maryknoll: Orbis Books, 1984.

Schmeiser, James (ed.). *Initiation Theology: Ecumenical Insights.* Toronto: The Anglican Book Centre, 1978.

Schmemann, Alexander. *For the Life of the World.* Crestwood, New York: St. Vladimir's Seminary Press, 1977.

Schmidt, Herman and Power, David (eds.). *Politics and Liturgy.* New York: Herder and Herder, 1974.

Searle, Mark (ed.). *Liturgy and Social Justice.* Collegeville: The Liturgical Press, 1980.

Seasoltz, R. Kevin (ed.). *Living Bread, Saving Cup: Readings on the Eucharist.* Collegeville: The Liturgical Press, 1982.

Senn, Frank C. *Christian Worship and its Cultural Setting.* Philadelphia: Fortress Press, 1983.

Sider, Ronald J. and Brubaker, Darrel J. (eds.). *Preaching on Peace.* Philadelphia: Fortress Press, 1982.

Skudlark, William. *The Word in Worship: Preaching in a Liturgical Context.* Nashville: Abingdon Press, 1981.

Soelle, Dorothee. *The Arms Race Kills Even Without War.* Philadelphia: Fortress Press, 1983.

Stringfellow, William. *The Politics of Spirituality.* Philadelphia: The Westminster Press, 1984.

This We Believe: The Symbols of the Lutheran Church. Minneapolis: Augsburg Publishing House, 1939.

Turner, Victor. *The Ritual Process: Structure and Anti-Structure.* Ithaca: Cornell University Press, 1969.

———. *Dramas, Fields, and Metaphors: Symbolic Action in Human Society.* Ithaca: Cornell University Press, 1974.

Vale, Norman. *Signs of the Times: Resources for Social Faith.* Toronto: The United Church of Canada, 1981.

Wainwright, Geoffrey. *Doxology: The Praise of God in Worship, Doctrine, and Life.* New York: Oxford University Press, 1980.

———. *Eucharist and Eschatology.* New York: Oxford University Press, 1981.

Wee, Paul A. *Systemic Injustice and the Biblical Witness.* Geneva: Lutheran World Federation, 1984.

Weil, Louis. *Sacraments and Liturgy: The Outward Signs.* Oxford: Basil Blackwell, 1980.

What Will We Do? Songs of Hunger and Justice. Philadelphia: Division for Parish Services, Lutheran Church in America, 1983.

White, James F. *Sacraments as God's Self Giving.* Nashville: Abingdon Press, 1983.

Willimon, William H. *The Service of God: How Worship and Ethics Are Related.* Nashville: Abingdon Press, 1983.

———. *Worship as Pastoral Care.* Nashville: Abingdon Press, 1979.

Worgul Jr., George. *From Magic to Metaphor: A Validation of the Christian Sacraments.* New York: Paulist Press, 1980.

Worship Among Lutherans. Geneva: Lutheran World Federation, 1983.

A Worship Book. Geneva: World Council of Churches, 1984.

B. Articles and Journals

Allen, Pamela Payne. *Taking the Next Step in Inclusive Language.* The Christian Century, April 23, 1986, pp. 410–413.

Beckman, Betsy. *Liturgical Dance and Liberation.* Liturgy, Vol. 5, No. 3, Winter, 1986.

Bourgeault, Cynthia. *Anti-Semitism in Our Musical Heritage.* Living Worship, Vol. 15, No. 9, November, 1979.

———. *Reawakening of a Sacramental Vision.* Living Worship, Vol. 15, No. 1, January, 1979.

Brand, Eugene L. *Baptism and Communion of Infants: A Lutheran View.* Worship, Vol. 50, No. 1, January 1976, pp. 29–42.

Brooks, Robert. *The Great Feast, Fount of Justice.* Liturgy, Vol. 2, No. 1, Spring, 1983.

Brown, Robert McAfee. *Spirituality and Liberation: The Case for Gustavo Gutierrez.* Worship, Vol. 58, No. 5, September, 1984, pp. 395–404.

Burchfield, Brian and Susan. *The Sunday Assembly as Gospel Event.* Liturgy, Vol. 2, No. 3, Winter, 1983.

Buttrick, David G. *Preaching the Christian Faith.* Liturgy, Vol. 2, No. 3, Winter 1983.

Collins, Mary. *Catechesis and Sunday Eucharist.* Liturgy 80, April 1982.

———. *Ritual Symbols and the Ritual Process: The Work of Victor W. Turner.* Worship, Vol. 50, No. 4, July, 1976, pp. 336–346.

Cone, James H. *Sanctification, Liberation and Black Worship.* Theology Today, Vol. XXXV, No. 2, July, 1978, pp. 139–152.

Cook, Guillermo. *The Relationship of Worship and Social Transformation in the Base Communities.* Reformed Liturgy and Music, pp. 89–92.

Crum Jr., Milton. *Preaching: What I Am About.* Worship, Vol. 50, No. 3, May, 1976, pp. 194–206.

Dallen, J. *The Social Activist-Liturgist Confrontation.* Today's Parish. Vol. 9, No. 4, April 1977, pp. 44–45.

DeClercq, Bertrand. *Political Commitment and Liturgical Celebration,* in *Political Commitment and Christian Community,* edited by Alois Muller and Norbert Greinacher. New York: Herder and Herder, 1973, pp. 110–116.

Deitering, Carolyn. *A Space for Liturgical Action.* Liturgy, Vol. 3, No. 4, Fall 1983.

Donaldson, Grace M. *The Non-Verbal Languages of Prayer.* Liturgy, Vol. 4, No. 4, Spring 1985.

Duba, Arlo D. *Hints for a Morphology of Eucharistic Praying: A Study of John 13:31–17:26.* Worship, Vol. 57, No. 4, July, 1983, pp. 365–377.

Egan, John. *Liturgy and Justice: An Unfinished Agenda.* Origins, Vol. 13, No. 15, September 22, 1983, pp. 245–253.

Evans, Bernard. *The Rural Parish: A Just and Caring Church.* Worship, Vol. 60, No. 5, September 1986, pp. 399–411.

Fink, Peter E. *Three Languages of Christian Sacraments.* Worship, Vol. 52, No. 6, November 1978, pp. 561–575.

124

Frohlich, Mary. *Politics, Mysticism and Liturgy. Liturgy,* Vol. 5, No. 3, Winter 1986.

Galvan, Michael. *Enculturating the Liturgy in North America. Liturgy,* Vol. 5, No. 3, Winter 1986.

Gelineau, Joseph. *Celebrating the Paschal Liberation,* in *Politics and Liturgy.* ed. Herman Schmidt and David Power. New York: Herder and Herder, 1974, pp. 107–119.

Gonzalez, Justo L. *Liturgy and Politics: A Latin American Perspective. Missiology,* Vol. 11, No. 2, April, 1974, pp. 175–182.

Grabner, John. *Ordained and Lay: Them-Us or We? Worship,* Vol. 54, No. 4, July, 1980, pp. 325–331.

Grindal, Gracia. *The Language of Worship and Hymnody: Tone. Worship,* Vol. 52, No. 6, November, 1978, pp. 509–517.

Gusmer, Charles W. *Is It WORSHIP? Evaluating the Sunday Eucharist. Living Worship,* Vol. 14, No. 10, December 1978.

Healey, Joseph G. *Inculturation of Liturgy and Worship in Africa. Worship,* Vol. 60, No. 5, September, 1986, pp. 412–423.

Hellwig, Monika K. *Transforming Power of the Eucharist. National Bulletin on Liturgy,* Vol. 15, No. 82, January–February 1982, pp. 43–48.

Henderson, J. Frank. *Bread and Wine, the Eucharistic Bread. Liturgy,* Vol. 2, No. 1, Spring 1982.

———. *Discrimination Against the Laity in Liturgical Texts and Rites. National Bulletin on Liturgy,* Vol. 20, No. 107, January–February 1987, pp. 51–60.

———. *The Minister of Liturgical Preaching. Worship,* Vol. 56, No. 3, May, 1982, pp. 214–230.

———. *The Names and Images of God. Liturgy,* Vol. 4, No. 4, Spring, 1985.

———. *When Lay People Preside at Sunday Worship. Worship,* Vol. 58, No. 2, March, 1984, pp. 108–117.

Higgins, George G. *The Mass and Political Order,* in *The New Ritual: Liturgy and Social Order.* Elsberry, Missouri: The Liturgical Conference, 1956.

Hoffman, Lawrence A. *Assembling in Worship. Worship,* Vol. 56, No. 2, March, 1982, pp. 98–112.

Hovda, Robert. *Adapting Liturgy in the United States: Sacred Function–Revolutionary Scene. Living Worship,* Vol. 7, No. 8, October, 1971.

———. *AIDS Hysteria and the Common Cup: Take and Drink.* The Amen Corner. *Worship,* Vol. 60, No. 1, January, 1986, pp. 67–73.

———. *Arid Work? Abstract Ideas? On Fostering Seven Cardinal Feelings in Liturgy Workers. Living Worship,* Vol. 12, No. 7, August–September, 1976.

———. *Baptismal Initiation and a Broader, Deeper Vision of the Church. Living Worship,* Vol. 5, No. 2, February, 1969.

———. *"Celebration of Man's Hope"—Liturgy and Permanent Unrest. Living Worship,* Vol. 5, No. 4, April, 1969.

———. *"Communion in the Hand"—A Small Gesture With a Potentially Large Significance. Living Worship,* Vol. 13, No. 7, August–September, 1977.

———. *". . . a Drop of the Bucket . . . Dust on the Scales"—Presuming to Pray During the 1976 Bicentennial. Living Worship,* Vol. 11, No. 8, October, 1975.

———. *"Environment and Art in Catholic Worship"— Bishops Stress the Primacy of the Assembly. Living Worship,* Vol. 14, No. 3, March, 1978.

———. *"The Ethical Demands of the Eucharist"— Reflections on the Context of Celebration. Living Worship,* Vol. 14, No. 7, August–September, 1978.

———. *The Eucharistic Prayer Is More Than Words. Living Worship,* Vol. 11, No. 4, April, 1975.

———. *"Kingdom Liturgy."* Unpublished manuscript.

———. *Let's Curb Visual Pollution!—The Environment of Worship. Living Worship,* Vol. 6, No. 5, May, 1970.

———. *Liturgical Celebration, the Person and Psychological Health—Part I. Living Worship,* Vol. 7, No. 9, November, 1971.

———. *Liturgical Celebration, the Person and Psychological Health—Part II. Living Worship,* Vol. 7, No. 10, December, 1971.

———. *Liturgy as Kingdom Play.* Chronicle. *Worship,* Vol. 56, No. 5, May, 1982.

———. *The Mass and Its Social Consequences. Liturgy 80,* June/July 1982.

———. *"Money or Gifts for the Poor and the Church."* The Amen Corner. *Worship,* Vol. 59, No. 1, January, 1985, pp. 65–71.

———. *The More Relevant Liturgy Is, The More Subversive It Is! Living Worship,* Vol. 6, No. 8, October, 1970.

———. *Not on Bread Alone Shall We Live. Liturgy,* Vol. 5, No. 4, Spring, 1986.

———. *Personal Experience in Prayer and the Insufficiency of Words. Living Worship,* Vol. 8, No. 1, January, 1972.

———. *Preparation, Formality and Style: Requirements of Liturgical Experience. Living Worship,* Vol. 9, No. 8, October, 1973.

———. *The Saving Evangelism of Our Symbol Language.* The Amen Corner. *Worship,* Vol. 58, No. 6, November, 1984, pp. 531–536.

———. *Scripture Has It, Not on Bread Alone Shall Human Creatures Live.* The Amen Corner. *Worship,* Vol. 57, No. 3, May, 1983, pp. 255–263.

———. *To Recall and to Renew the Ancient Memories.* The Amen Corner. *Worship,* Vol. 60, No. 3, May, 1986, pp. 246–254.

———. *The What and Why of Liturgy. Living Worship,* Vol. 10, No. 9, November 1974.

———. *Where Have You Been? "Peace Liturgies" Are the Only Kind We Have!* The Amen Corner. *Worship,* Vol. 57, No. 5, September 1983, pp. 438–443.

———. *Without . . . Solidarity and Justice . . . Celebration Is an Empty Action . . ." Living Worship,* Vol. 9, No. 3, March, 1973.

———. *Women in Ministry?—We Breathe, We Spit, We Are! Living Worship,* Vol. 6, No. 3, March 1970.

Huck, Gabe. *The Role of Liturgical Celebration in Fostering Spiritual Growth. Living Worship,* Vol. 14, No. 6, June–July, 1978.

Huffman, Walter C. *The Concept of Sacred Space. Liturgy*, Vol. 5, No. 4, Spring 1986.

Jegen, Carol Frances. *Communion in Peace and Justice. Liturgy*, Vol. 5, No. 2, Fall 1985.

———. *The Eucharist and Peacemaking: Sign of Contradiction? Worship*, Vol. 59, No. 3, May 1985, pp. 202–210.

Jegen, Mary Evelyn. *Theology and Spirituality of Nonviolence. Worship*, Vol. 60, No. 2, March, 1986, pp. 119–133.

Jenson, Robert W. *The Eucharist: For Infants? Living Worship*, Vol. 15, No. 6, June–July, 1979.

Judd, Peter A. *Children and the Art of Worship. Liturgy*, Vol. 4, No. 4, Spring 1985.

Keenan, Joseph. *The Importance of the Creation Motif in a Eucharistic Prayer. Worship*, Vol. 53, No. 4, July, 1979, pp. 341–356.

Keifer, Ralph A. *Now the Sacred Words Are Done: Liturgy in a Post-Translation Era. Living Worship*, Vol. 12, No. 5, May 1976.

Kellermann, Bill. *The Political Geography of Prayer. Liturgy*, Vol. 5, No. 1, Summer 1985.

Kennedy, Dennis. *The Sacrament of Footwashing: I Have Set You an Example. Living Worship*, Vol. 16, No. 2, February, 1980.

Kiesling, Christopher. *Liturgy and Consumerism. Worship*, Vol. 52, No. 4, July, 1978, pp. 359–368.

———. *Liturgy and Social Justice. Worship*, Vol. 51, No. 4, July 1977, pp. 351–361.

———. *Liturgy Call to Social Justice. Modern Liturgy*, Vol. 7, No. 5, August 1980.

———. *Social Justice and the Eucharist. New Catholic World*, Vol. 224, No. 1342, July/August 1981, pp. 173–177.

Kodell, Jerome. *The Word in Christian Liturgy. Liturgy*, Vol. 2, No. 3, Winter 1980.

Lane, Dermot A. *The Eucharist and Social Justice*, in *Eucharist for a New World*, edited by Sean Swayne. Carlow, Ireland: Irish Institute of Pastoral Liturgy, 1981, pp. 55–68.

Lardner, Gerald V. *Sign and Symbol in the Eucharist, New Catholic World*, Vol. 224, No. 1342, July/August, 1981, pp. 169–172.

Larson, Rebecca S. *Drumbeats and Deep Longings. The United Church Observer*, April 1983.

Larson, Stephen M. *Old Ruins and New Images. Liturgy*, Vol. 3, No. 4, Fall 1983.

Lathrop, Gordon W. *The Eucharist as a "Hungry Feast" and the Appropriateness of Our Want. Living Worship*, Vol. 13, No. 9, September 1977.

———. *Liturgy: Pattern and Image for Ministry. Liturgy*, Vol. 22, No. 7, November 1977, pp. 28–32.

———. *A Rebirth of Images. Worship*, Vol. 58, No. 4, July 1984, pp. 291–304.

———. *Scripture in the Assembly: The Ancient and Lively Tension. Liturgy*, Vol. 2, No. 3, Summer 1982.

Laverdiere, Eugene. *Eucharist as Proclamation, Liberation Communion*, in *Eucharist for a New World*, edited by Sean Swayne. Carlow, Ireland: Irish Institute of Pastoral Liturgy, 1981, pp. 69–72.

LeCroy, Anne. *Overcoming Sexism in Worship. Liturgy*, Vol. 4, No. 4, Spring 1985.

Lehmann, Paul. *Praying and Doing Justly. Reformed Liturgy and Music*, pp. 77–81.

Liturgy and Peace. Assembly. Notre Dame: Notre Dame Center for Pastoral Liturgy, Vol. 11, No. 3, February, 1985.

Liturgy and Social Action. Assembly. Notre Dame: Notre Dame Center for Pastoral Liturgy, Vol. 6, No. 1, June 1979.

Llopis, Joan. *The Message of Liberation in the Liturgy*, in *Politics and Liturgy*. Ed. Herman Schmidt and David Power. New York: Herder and Herder, 1974, pp. 65–73.

Luebring, Carol. *Welcoming Children to the Table. Liturgy*, Vol. 5, No. 1, Summer 1985.

Maher, Mary C. *Is the Christian Community Responsible for the Liturgical Preaching it Hears? Living Worship*, Vol. 13, No. 8, October 1977.

Mahony, Roger. *The Eucharist and Social Justice. Worship*, Vol. 57, No. 1, January 1983, pp. 52–61.

Malarcher, Willy. *The Climate of Worship. Liturgy*, Vol. 5, No. 4, Spring 1986.

Manly, Greg. *Teach Us To Pray. Living Worship*, Vol. 16, No. 1, January 1980.

Marshall, Paul V. *The Liturgy of Preaching. Liturgy*, Vol. 1, No. 4, Spring 1982.

Mauck, Marchita B. *Buildings That House the Church. Liturgy*, Vol. 5, No. 4, Spring 1986.

McDiarmid, M. *First Do Justice, Then Celebrate. Pastoral Music*, August–September, 1981.

McKenna, John H. *Liturgy: Toward Liberation or Oppression? Worship*, Vol. 56, No. 4, July 1982, pp. 291–308.

McManus, Frederick R. *The Setting for Christian Worship. Liturgy*, Vol. 5, No. 4, Spring 1986.

Metz, Johannes B. *The Future in the Memory of Suffering*, in *New Questions on God*, Ed. J. B. Metz. New York: Herder and Herder, 1972, pp. 9–25.

Meyer, Hans Bernhard. *The Social Significance of the Liturgy*, in *Politics and Liturgy*. Ed. Herman Schmidt and David Power. New York: Herder and Herder, 1974, pp. 34–50.

Mitchell, Nathan. *Bread of Crisis, Bread of Justice. Living Worship*, Vol. 15, No. 3, March 1979.

———. *"Symbols are Actions, Not Objects"—New Directions for an Old Problem. Living Worship*, Vol. 13, No. 2, February 1977.

Moiser, J. *A Promise of Plenty: The Eucharist as Social Critique. The Downside Review*, Vol. 91, No. 305, October, 1973.

Moltmann, Jurgen. *The Liberating Feast*, in *Politics and Liturgy*, Ed. Herman Schmidt and David Power. New York: Herder and Herder, 1974, pp. 74–84.

Neuhaus, Richard John. *Liturgy and the Politics of the Kingdom. The Christian Century*, December 20, 1967, pp. 1623–1627.

Ng, David. *Children in the Worshiping Community. Liturgy*, Vol. 1, No. 3, Summer 1982.

Norris Jr., Richard A. *The Ordination of Women and the*

"Maleness" of Christ. *Living Worship*, Vol. 13, No. 3, March 1977.

Northup, Lesley Armstrong. *The Woman as Presider: Images Drawn from Life. Worship*, Vol. 58, No. 6, November, 1984, pp. 526–530.

Notebaart, James. *The Font and the Assembly. Liturgy*, Vol. 5, No. 4, Spring 1986.

———. *Reflections on the Symbols of the Easter Vigil. Living Worship*, Vol. 11, No. 2, February 1975.

———. *Shaping the Environment of Celebration: Art, Design for Visual Order and Beauty. Living Worship*, Vol. 10, No. 3, March 1974.

O'Connor, Jerome Murphy. *Eucharist and Community in First Corinthians. Worship*, Vol. 50, No. 5, September, 1976, pp. 370–385 (Part I); Vol. 51, No. 1, January, 1977, pp. 56–69 (Part II).

Pawlikowski, John T. *Worship After the Holocaust. Worship*, Vol. 58, No. 4, July 1984, pp. 315–341.

Pfatteicher, Philip H. *Worship: The Source and Summit of Faith. Consensus: A Canadian Lutheran Journal of Theology*, Vol. IX, No. 2, April 1983.

———. *Worship: The Source of Renewal. Consensus: A Canadian Lutheran Journal of Theology*, Vol. IX, No. 3, July, 1983.

Power, David. *The Song of the Lord in an Alien Land, in Politics and Liturgy.* Ed. Herman Schmidt and David Power. New York: Herder and Herder, 1974, pp. 85–106.

Rambusch, Robert. *Creating a House for the Church. Liturgy*, Vol. 5, No. 4, Spring 1986.

Ramshaw, Elaine. *Sacramental Readiness and Psychology. Liturgy*, Vol. 1, No. 3, Winter 1982.

Ramshaw-Schmidt, Gail. *Catechesis for Baptized Children. Liturgy*, Vol. 4, No. 1, Winter 1985.

———. *De Divinis Nominibus: The Gender of God. Worship*, Vol. 56, No. 2, March 1982, pp. 117–131.

———. *The Language of Eucharistic Praying. Worship*, Vol. 57, No. 5, September 1983, pp. 419–437.

———. *Liturgy as Poetry: Implications of a Definition. Living Worship*, Vol. 15, No. 8, October 1979.

———. *Lutheran Liturgical Prayer And God as Mother. Worship*, Vol. 52, No. 6, November 1978, pp. 517–542.

———. *The Word in the World. Consensus: A Canadian Lutheran Journal of Theology*, Vol. VIII, No. 4, October 1982.

Riegert, Eduard R. *Worship. Consensus: A Canadian Lutheran Journal of Theology*, Vol. XI, No. 2, April 1985.

———. *Worship and the Church's Mission. Consensus: A Canadian Lutheran Journal of Theology*, Vol. IX, No. 1, January 1983.

Rouillard, Philippe. *From Human Meal to Christian Eucharist. Worship*, Vol. 52, No. 5, September 1978, pp. 425–439 (Part I); Vol. 53, No. 1, January 1979, pp. 40–56 (Part II).

Routley, Erik. *The Gender of God: A Contribution to the Conversation. Worship*, Vol. 56, No. 3, May 1982, pp. 231–239.

———. *Sexist Language: A View From a Distance. Worship*, Vol. 53, No. 1, January 1979, pp. 2–11.

Rowthorn, Jeffrey. *Hail to the Lord's Anointed: Justice in the Church's Hymn of Praise. Modern Liturgy*, Vol. 7, No. 5, August 1980.

Ryan, John Barry. *Preparing a Global Perspective in Liturgical Studies. Worship*, Vol. 60, No. 4, July 1986, pp. 291–304.

Saliers, Don E. *Language in the Liturgy: Where Angels Fear to Tread. Worship*, Vol. 52, No. 6, November 1978, pp. 482–488.

———. *Symbol in Liturgy: Tracing the Hidden Languages. Worship*, Vol. 58, No. 1, January 1984, pp. 37–48.

Sawicki, Marianne. *Ministry of the Word—Without Sexism. Living Worship*, Vol. 15, No. 2, February 1979.

Schlichting, Janet. *Holy People Make Holy Places. Liturgy*, Vol. 3, No. 4, Fall 1983.

Schmid, Vernon. *Our Gift of Freedom: The Eucharist and Justice. Liturgy*, Vol. 2, No. 1, Spring 1982.

Schultz, Gustav H. *Does That Mean the Celebrant Is a Politician? Modern Liturgy*, Vol. 7, No. 5, August 1980.

Searle, Mark. *The Pedagogical Function of the Liturgy. Worship*, Vol. 55, No. 4, July 1981, pp. 332–359.

———. *The Uses of Liturgical Language. Liturgy*, Vol. 4, No. 4, Spring 1985.

Seasoltz, R. Kevin. *Justice and the Eucharist. Worship*, Vol. 58, No. 6, November 1984, pp. 507–525.

———. *Peace: Belief, Prayer and Life. Worship*, Vol. 56, No. 2, March 1982, pp. 152–172.

———. *Proclaiming God's Word, Speaking God's Name. Liturgy*, Vol. 4, No. 4, Spring 1985.

Senn, Frank C. *Church Year Calendars and Lectionaries. Living Worship*, Vol. 16, No. 9, November 1980.

———. *Sacred Meals and Gracious Dining. Liturgy*, Vol. 2, No. 1, Summer 1983.

Sloyan, Gerard S. *The Lectionary as a Context for Interpretation. Liturgy*, Vol. 2, No. 3, Winter 1983.

Smith, Gregory. *Values and Uses of Silence as Part of Liturgical Action. Living Worship*, Vol. 13, No. 5, May 1977.

Smith Jr., Luther E. *Spirituality and Social Freedom. Liturgy*, Vol. 5, No. 3, Winter 1986.

Social Justice. Modern Liturgy, Vol. 7, No. 5, August 1980 (entire issue).

Sovik, Edward A. *Church Architecture—A Public Language. Liturgy*, Vol. 4, No. 4, Spring 1985.

Stauffer, S. Anita. *A Place for Burial, Birth and Bath. Liturgy*, Vol. 5, No. 4, Spring 1986.

Stevick, Daniel B. *The Language of Prayer. Worship*, Vol. 52, No. 6, November 1978, pp. 542–560.

Szews, George R. *Ministers of Hospitality and Greeting. Liturgy*, Vol. 1, No. 4, Spring 1982.

Talley, Thomas J. *From Berakah to Eucharistia: A Reopening Question. Worship*, Vol. 50, No. 2, March 1976, pp. 115–137.

Thompson, Mikkel. *The Presence of Christ in the Word. Liturgy*, Vol. 2, No. 3, Winter 1983.

Toporoski, Richard. *The Language of Worship. Worship*, Vol. 52, No. 6, November 1978, pp. 489–508.

Turner, Victor. *Passages, Margins and Poverty: Religious*

Symbols of Communitas. Worship, Vol. 46, No. 7, August–September 1972, pp. 390–412 (Part I); Vol. 46, No. 8, October 1972, pp. 482–494 (Part II).

———. *Ritual, Tribal and Catholic. Worship,* Vol. 50, No. 6, November 1976, pp. 504–526.

Vannucchi, Aldo. *Liturgy and Liberation. International Review of Missions,* Vol. LXV, No. 258, April 1976, pp. 186–195.

Wainwright, Geoffrey. *Between God and World: Worship and Mission,* in *Liturgy Reshaped: Festschrift for Geoffrey Cumming,* edited by K. Stevenson. London: S.P.C.K., 1979.

Walsh, David W. *Social Justice and Liturgy in Contemporary Spirituality. Modern Liturgy,* Vol. 7, No. 5, August 1980.

Weber, Joseph C. *The Eucharist, A Political Parable. Liturgy,* Vol. 4, No. 4, Spring 1985.

Weil, Louis. *Liturgy and Its Social Dimensions,* in *Sacraments and Liturgy: The Outward Signs.* Oxford: Basil Blackwell, 1980.

———. *Liturgy in a Disintegrating World. Worship,* Vol. 54, No. 4, July 1980, pp. 291–302.

White, James F. *Coming Together in Christ's Name. Liturgy,* Vol. 1, No. 4, Summer 1982.

———. *Liturgy and the Language of Space. Worship,* Vol. 52, No. 1, January 1978, pp. 57–66.

———. *Worship as a Source of Injustice. Reformed Liturgy and Music,* pp. 72–76.

Willimon, William H. *The Peace of God Go With You. Liturgy,* Vol. 1, No. 4, Summer 1982.

Winter, Miriam Therese. *Sing If You Know Justice. Liturgy,* Vol. 5, No. 1, Summer 1985.

Wolterstorff, Nicholas. *Worship and Justice. Reformed Liturgy and Music,* pp. 67–71.

Wren, Brian. *Justice and Liberation in the Eucharist. The Christian Century,* October 1, 1986, p. 839–842.

Notes

Scripture. Quotations from the Bible are taken from the Revised Standard Version.

Liturgical Books are referred to by the following abbreviations.

Anglican/Episcopal

BAS   *The Book of Alternative Services of The Anglican Church of Canada* (Toronto: Anglican Book Centre 1985)

BCP   *The Book of Common Prayer and Administration of the Sacraments and Other Rites and Ceremonies of the Church, Together with The Psalter or Psalms of David, According to the Use of The Episcopal Church* (New York: Church Hymnal Corporation 1980)

Lutheran

LBW   *Lutheran Book of Worship.* Ministers Desk Edition (Minneapolis: Augsburg Publishing House 1978)

Roman Catholic

RB   "Rite of Baptism," in *The Rites of the Catholic Church as Revised by Decree of the Second Vatican Ecumenical Council and Published by Authority of Pope Paul VI* (New York: Pueblo Publishing Co. 1976)

RM   *Sacramentary: The Roman Missal revised by Decree of the Second Vatican Ecumenical Council and Published by Authority of Pope Paul VI* (Ottawa: Canadian Catholic Conference 1974, 1983). Roman Catholic liturgical texts in English are copyrighted by the International Commission on English in the Liturgy, Washington, DC

GB   *Eucharistic Prayers for Study and Comment* ("Green Book") (Washington: International Commission on English in the Liturgy 1980)

United Church of Canada

SB   *Service Book for the Use of Ministers Conducting Public Worship* (Toronto: The Ryerson Press for the United Church of Canada 1969)

SL   *A Sunday Liturgy for Optional Use in The United Church of Canada* (Toronto: Working Unit on Worship and Liturgy, Division of Mission in Canada 1984)

We also often quote from: *Baptism, Eucharist, and Ministry* (Geneva: World Council of Churches 1982)

1. Introduction

1. Joseph Gelineau, "Celebrating the Paschal Liberation," in H. Schmidt and D. N. Power, eds., *Politics and Liturgy* (Concilium 92) (New York: Herder & Herder 1974) p. 107.
2. Desmond Tutu, in *Freedom Is Coming, Songs of Protest and Praise from South Africa* (Uppsala: Utryk 1984) p. 22.
3. Delia Carley, "Bread Broken and Shared Brings Life to Christian Community," *Catholic New Times* (Toronto) September 16, 1984, p. 11.
4. Paul De Groot, *The Edmonton Journal* (Edmonton), January 17, 1986.
5. Ernesto Cardenal, *The Gospel in Solentiname* (Maryknoll: Orbis Books 1980), pp. 165–167.
6. "Lord, Make Us Hungry . . . Make Us Bread," *Bread for the World Worship Aids II* (Chicago: Bread for the World Educational Fund), p. 11.
7. Doris Janzen Longacre, *Living More With Less* (Kitchener: Herald Press 1980), p. 239.
8. Mary Pope, "What Language Shall I Borrow? Worship in Times of Crisis" unpublished paper presented to the Working Group on Liturgy and Social Justice of the North American Academy on Liturgy, January 1987.
9. Name withheld. Response solicited by the authors.
10. *Ibid.*
11. *The Ploughshares Monitor* (Vol. 8, No. 2, June 1987), p. 1.
12. Paul De Groot, *The Edmonton Journal* (Edmonton), January 10, 1987.
13. Ernesto Cardenal, *The Gospel in Solentiname* (Maryknoll: Orbis Books 1980), pp. 147–148.

2. Liturgy's Call to Social Justice

1. *CCA News*, a publication of the Christian Conference of Asia, in *Scarboro Missions Magazine* (July–August 1987), p. 16.
2. "The Empty Place" (Franciscan Communications Centre 1976), in Meredith Sommers Dregni, *Experiencing More With Less* (Kitchener: Herald Press, 1983), p. 100.
3. Mary Martin, in Doris Longacre, *Living More With Less* (Kitchener: Herald Press 1980), p. 86.
4. Tad Guzie, *Sacramental Basics* (New York: Paulist Press 1981), p. 10.
5. Judith Mattison, in Meredith Sommers Dregni, *Experiencing More With Less* (Kitchener: Herald Press 1983), p. 44.
6. Source unknown.
7. *The Ploughshares Monitor* (Vol. 8, no. 2, June 1987), p. 1.

8. Source unknown.

9. John Paul II, "A Defense of the Rights of Aborigines," *Origins* (Dec. 11, 1986), pp. 473, 475.

10. Leslie Brandt, in Meredith Sommers Dregni, *Experiencing More with Less* (Kitchener: Herald Press 1983), p. 75.

11. Source unknown.

12. Ronald J. Sider, in Meredith Sommers Dregni, *Experiencing More With Less* (Kitchener: Herald Press 1983), pp. 76–77.

13. Helder Camara, *The Desert Is Fertile* (Maryknoll: Orbis Books 1974), p. 27.

14. *Ibid.*

15. Linda and David Norman, in Doris Janzen Longacre, *Living More With Less* (Kitchener: Herald Press 1980), p. 280.

16. Waldron Scott, in Doris Janzen Longacre, *Living More With Less* (Kitchener: Herald Press 1980), p. 235.

17. Christopher Kiesling, "Liturgy: Call to Social Justice," *Modern Liturgy* (Vol. 7, August 1980), p. 37.

18. Rene Fumoleau, "Yellowknife, N.W.T.," unpublished poem, 1986, used with permission.

19. Matthew Fox, *Original Blessing* (Bear & Co., 1983), p. 145.

20. Geoffrey Wainwright, *Doxology: The Praise of God in Worship, Doctrine and Life* (New York: Oxford University Press), p. 8.

3. Principles of Liturgy and Social Justice

1. John Egan, "Liturgy and Social Justice: We've Only Just Begun," *Origins* (Vol. 13, September 1983), p. 245.

2. Virgil Michel, quoted by John Egan, *op. cit.*, p. 252.

3. *Ibid.*

4. *Ibid.*

5. *A Lutheran Agenda for Worship* (Geneva: Lutheran World Federation, 1979), p. 10.

6. Pamela Payne Allen, "Taking the Next Step in Inclusive Language," *The Christian Century* (April 23, 1986), p. 411.

7. "The Kairos Document" (Braamfontein 2017, South Africa, 1985).

8. BAS, Eucharistic Prayer 3, p. 198; BCP, Eucharistic Prayer B, p. 386.

9. BAS, Eucharistic Prayer 4, p. 201; BCP, Eucharistic Prayer C, p. 370; SL, Eucharistic Prayer 4, p. 25.

10. LBW, Great Thanksgiving 1, p. 221.

11. SL, Eucharistic Prayer 6, p. 32.

12. RM, Preface for Sundays V.

13. BAS, Eucharistic Prayer 1, p. 193.

14. SL, Eucharistic Prayer 3, p. 22.

15. BAS, Eucharistic Prayer 2, p. 196.

16. BAS, Eucharistic Prayer 5, p. 205.

17. RM, Eucharistic Prayer IV.

18. RM, Eucharistic Prayer for Masses of Reconciliation 2.

19. John Egan, *op. cit.*, p. 247.

20. Mark Searle, "Serving the Lord with Justice," in *Liturgy and Social Justice*, edited by Mark Searle (Collegeville, MN: Liturgical Press, 1980), pp. 17–18.

21. *Ibid.*, pp. 16–17.

22. John Egan, *op. cit.*, p. 251.

23. Martin E. Marty, "State of Emergency: Church Testimony," *Christian Century*, Vol. 103, no. 26 (Sept. 10, 1986), p. 765.

24. GB, Eucharistic Prayer 4, p. 24.

25. *Worship Among Lutherans* (Geneva: Lutheran World Federation, 1983).

26. *Eucharistic Prayers for Study and Comment* (Washington: International Commission on English in the Liturgy, 1980), pp. 64–67.

27. *Preparing by Prayer* (Ottawa: Canadian Conference of Catholic Bishops, 1983), *passim*.

28. John Kavanagh, *Following Christ in a Consumer Society* (Maryknoll: Orbis Books, 1981), p. 15.

29. *Third World Solidarity Day, Share Lent '87* (Toronto: Canadian Catholic Organization for Development and Peace, 1987), p. 24.

4. The Gathering of God's People

1. BAS, Preface for the Lord's Day 2, p. 218.

2. Aidan Kavanagh, *Elements of Rite* (New York: Pueblo Publishing Co., 1982), p. 28.

3. RM, Eucharistic Prayer IV.

4. RM, Eucharistic Prayer III.

5. Anders Nyberg, *Freedom Is Coming: Songs of Protest and Praise* (Uppsala: Utryk 1984), p. 4.

6. Justin Martyr, *Apology* I, 67.

7. RM, Preface for Sundays I.

8. SL, Eucharistic Prayer 6, p. 34.

9. Frederic Debuyst, *Modern Architecture and Christian Celebration* (London: Lutterworth Press, 1968), p. 31.

10. *An Old Gaelic Rune* (Dublin: The Cuala Press, no date).

11. *Didiscalia of the Apostles* 12.

12. Bob Crepeau in Doris Janzen Longacre, *Living More With Less* (Kitchner: Herald Press, 1980), pp. 239–240.

13. David Newman, *As Often As You Do This* (Toronto: Division of Mission in Canada, United Church of Canada, 1981), pp. 40–41.

14. *Music in Catholic Worship* (Washington: U.S. Catholic Conference, 1972), p. 5.

15. RM, Order of Mass; LBW, Holy Communion, p. 196; BAS, The Gathering of the Community, p. 185.

16. BAS, The Gathering of the Community, p. 185; BCP, The Word of God, p. 335.

17. BAS, The Gathering of the Community, p. 185.

18. LBW, Brief Order for Confession and Forgiveness, p. 195.

19. RM, Order of Mass.

20. LBW, The Holy Innocents, Prayer of the Day, p. 172.

21. LBW, The Fourth Sunday of Easter, Prayer of the Day, p. 155.

5. The Liturgy of the Word

1. SL, Eucharistic Prayer 2, p. 20.
2. RM, Eucharistic Prayer for Reconciliation 2.
3. BAS, Eucharistic Prayer 2, p. 196.
4. Ernesto Cardenal, *The Gospel in Solentiname* (Maryknoll: Orbis Books, 1980), p. 51.
5. SL, Eucharistic Prayer 6, p. 32.
6. BAS, Eucharistic Prayer 4, p. 201.
7. Egan, *op. cit.,* p. 251.
8. Egan, *op. cit.,* p. 252.
9. Robert W. Hovda, "The Mass and Its Social Consequences," *Liturgy 80,* June/July 1982, p. 5.
10. Robert W. Hovda, *Dry Bones* (Washington: The Liturgical Conference, 1973), p. 73.
11. Justin Martyr, *Apology* I, 67.
12. LBW, p. 201.
13. BAS, The Proclamation of the Word, p. 187; SL, p. 8.
14. RM, The Liturgy of the Word.
15. BAS, The Proclamation of the Word, p. 188; SL, p. 9.
16. LBW, p. 202.
17. Oscar Romero, quoted in *Compass,* No. 1 (1983), p. 18.
18. William Wipfler, quoted in *Newsletter of the Inter-Church Committee on Human Rights in Latin America* (Toronto) July/August 1980, p. 36.
19. Walter Burghardt, "Preaching the Just Word," *Liturgy and Social Justice,* ed. by Mark Searle (Collegeville: The Liturgical Press, 1980), pp. 36–52.
20. Vilmos Vajta, "Worship in a Secularized Age," *Worship and Secularization,* ed. by Wiebe Vos (Geneva: Commission on Faith and Order, World Council of Churches, 1970), p. 77.
21. Herbert Brokering, *"I" Opener* (St. Louis: Concordia Publishing House, 1974), p. 31.

6. The Liturgy of Baptism

1. LBW, Holy Baptism, p. 308.
2. SL, Eucharistic Prayer 1, p. 17.
3. Robert W. Hovda, "The Mass and Its Social Consequences," *Liturgy 80* (June–July 1982), p. 6.
4. T. S. Eliot, "Ash Wednesday," *The Complete Poems and Plays 1909–1950* (New York: Harcourt, Brace and World, 1971), p. 66.
5. Ralph Freeman, *Two Hymns and a Spiritual Song* (Minneapolis: Augsburg, 1986).
6. "Baptism," in *Baptism, Eucharist and Ministry* (Geneva: World Council of Churches, 1982).
7. Hippolytus of Rome, *The Apostolic Tradition,* 15, 16.
8. "Baptism," in *Baptism, Eucharist and Ministry, op. cit.*
9. Based on a talk by Joan Halmo (Saskatoon, Sask.).
10. BAS, Presentation and Examination of the Candidate, p. 153; BCP, Presentation and Examination of the Candidate, p. 302.

11. LBW, Holy Baptism, p. 309.
12. RB, Reception of the Children, p. 198.
13. BAS, Prayers for the Candidates, p. 155; BCP, Prayers for the Candidates, p. 305.
14. LBW, Holy Baptism, pp. 309–310.
15. BAS, Thanksgiving over the Water, pp. 157–158; BCP, Thanksgiving over the Water, pp. 306–307.
16. William E. Reiser, "Baptismal Promises: Making the Words Bite," *America* (February 22, 1986).
17. BAS, Presentation and Examination of the Candidate, p. 154; BCP, Presentation and Examination of the Candidate, p. 302.
18. BAS, The Baptismal Covenant, p. 159; BCP, The Baptismal Covenant, p. 304.
19. LBW, Holy Baptism, p. 312.
20. BAS, Welcome, p. 161.
21. LBW, p. 124.
22. RB, Clothing with White Garment, p. 209.
23. BAS, The Giving of Light, p. 160.

7. The Liturgy of the Eucharist

1. BAS, Thanksgiving Litany, p. 128.
2. BAS, General Thanksgiving Prayer, p. 129.
3. SL, Eucharistic Prayer 4, p. 27; BAS, Eucharistic Prayer 4, p. 203.
4. SL, Eucharistic Prayer 1, p. 18; SL, Eucharistic Prayer 6, p. 34.
5. BAS, Eucharistic Prayer 6, p. 208; BCP, Eucharistic Prayer 8, p. 374.
6. Martin Luther, "Treatise on the Blessed Sacrament" (1519).
7. Mark Searle *op. cit.* p. 27.
8. Jurgen Moltmann, quoted by Regis Duffy, "Symbols of Abundance, Symbols of Need," in Mark Searle, ed., *Liturgy and Social Justice* (Collegeville: Liturgical Press, 1986), p. 83.
9. Tissa Balasuriya, *The Eucharist and Human Liberation* (Maryknoll: Orbis Books 1979), pp. xi–xii.
10. Mary Collins, *op. cit.,* p. 5.
11. BAS, Eucharistic Prayer 5, p. 204; BCP, Eucharistic Prayer D, p. 373.
12. BAS, Eucharistic Prayer 6, p. 207.
13. BAS, Eucharistic Prayer 6, p. 208.
14. Louis Weil, *op. cit.* p. 99.
15. Sister M. Robison, quoted by John Koenig, *New Testament Hospitality* (Philadelphia: Fortress Press, 1985), p. 146.
16. Robert W. Hovda, "The Mass and Its Social Consequences," *op. cit.* p. 5.
17. Arthur Simon, "Hunger and Holy Communion," *Lutheran Forum* (April 1971), p. 9.
18. Tad Guzie, *What the Eucharist Means to Catholic Families* (Chicago: Claretian Publications, 1983), pp. 28–31.
19. LBW, Holy Communion, p. 206.
20. RM, Preparation of Gifts.
21. BAS, Sunday—Proper 14: Collect, p. 367.
22. *Prayers We Have in Common, op. cit.*

23. *Prayers We Have in Common, op. cit.*

24. RM, Eucharistic Acclamations A and B; BAS, Eucharistic Prayer 1, p. 199.

25. Krister Stendahl, from *Thy Kingdom Come: Report to the World Council of Churches Melbourne Consultation* (*Geneva: World Council of Churches*), pp. 81–82.

26. BAS, The Holy Eucharist, p. 212.

27. BAS, The Communion, p. 213; BCP, Holy Eucharist, p. 364; SL, p. 11.

28. LBW, Holy Communion, p. 263; SL, p. 11; RM, Order of Mass.

29. BAS, The Communion, p. 213; BCP, Holy Eucharist, p. 365; SL, p. 11.

30. Third World Solidarity Day Booklet, *op. cit.*

8. The Sending Forth of God's People

1. Arthur Simon, "Hunger and Holy Communion," *Lutheran Forum*, April 1971, p. 9.

2. Delia Carley, "Bread Broken and Shared Brings Life to a Christian Community," *Catholic New Times* (Toronto) (September 16, 1984) p. 11.

3. Dermot Lane, "The Eucharist and Social Justice," *Eucharist for a New World* (Carlow, Ireland: Irish Institute of Pastoral Liturgy, 1981), pp. 66–67.

4. Third World Solidarity Day Booklet, *op. cit.*, p. 29.

5. BAS, Sunday—Proper 14: Prayer after Communion, p. 367.

6. BAS, The Holy Innocents: Prayer after Communion, p. 399.

7. LBW, Holy Communion, p. 230; SB, p. 187.

8. RM, Order of Mass: Solemn Blessings.